POLE FISHING

First published in the UK 1992
by Boxtree Limited,
36 Tavistock Street,
London WC2E

1 3 5 7 9 10 8 6 4 2

Design by Paul Ewen
Editor: Helen Douglas-Cooper

Colour origination by Fotographics, Hong Kong
Printed in England by Clays Ltd, St Ives plc

A catalogue record for this book is available
from the British Library.

ISBN 1 85283 190 1

POLE FISHING

Edited by Kevin Wilmot
with a foreword by Jan Porter

BOXTREE

Elastic takes the strain as a carp bids for freedom.

CONTENTS

ACKNOWLEDGEMENTS

The editor and publishers would
like to thank the following:

Malcolm Lane for use of his illustrations

Bob Atkins, Angus Murray and Phil Bagnall
for use of their photographs.

Thanks also to all of the anglers who
have helped contribute to
Improve Your Coarse Fishing magazine
since its launch in 1991.

FOREWORD

Over the past 20 years the face of angling has changed beyond all recognition. Technology has heralded a new dawning in the manufacture of fishing accessories, which has benefitted anglers of all disciplines. However, the area where most of the benefit has been felt – and appreciated – is in pole fishing. Poles have been transformed from the heavy, floppy, glass-fibre versions of the 1960s and 1970s to the ultra-light, rigid carbon poles of today — and at an affordable price.

I was very lucky to be able to afford a top-notch pole as far back as 1981. Having just won the River Yare Championships that year, I soon converted the £525 winner's purse into a 10 m Daiwa Pro-carbon model, which set me back £400.

At that time I was one of only a handful of anglers in the Nottingham area to possess a pole made from this superb new material but I knew that to get ahead on the fiercely competitive local open-match circuit I would have to stay one step in front. Another reason was that I had endured a very unsettling experience in Ireland on a festival the previous May, when Leicester's Trev Tomlin, using a 10 m carbon pole, gave me one of the biggest next-peg thrashings of my whole career. I won't go into too much detail, but if I remember right I was about 140 lb in arrears.

I think it would also be fair to say that in our neck of the woods the pole caught on later than in the south or the north west of England, and as a result there was little information on pole fishing techniques at grass-roots level. Much of the pole angler's skills had to be obtained by trial and error. In fact, the first time I used one I tried to fish to-hand with a waggler, which was a complete disaster.

Quite clearly, there are days when the pole can be a devastating method in terms of fish-catching. However, that first session was devastating in a different way — I don't think I've ever had so many tangles in a day's fishing!

Gradually things started coming together as I progressed in the match world and discovered friends who passed on much-needed but basic tips, which I was to put into use. How I wish there had been a book like this one around at the time! One trick that helped me was always to practise with a pole if I had drawn a

MARCEL VAN DEN EYNDE
LOKAAS
AMORCE
GROUNDBAIT
PASTURA
3 X WORLD CHAMPION

bad area in a match. Surprisingly enough, I caught a lot of fish, won section prizes and even got into the main list on a few occasions.

Since then, one of the many highlights of my pole fishing career was when I caught 133 lb 12 oz of roach on Lough Erne in Northern Ireland in the Brennan and Hickman Open. I only managed third because my groundbait wasn't right, but Kevin Ashurst's certainly was and he won with a staggering 207 lb.

Whether you are using a 2 m or a 12 m pole, I can promise you lots of exciting times with this delightful style of fishing. I can't guarantee breaking the 100 lb barrier, but you will have plenty of fun along the way as you become more competent with the help of this book. The *Improve Your Coarse Fishing Book of Pole Fishing* brings the reader up to date on all aspects of the technique, and is suitable for both beginner and expert alike. I wholeheartedly recommend it.

As the saying goes, practice makes perfect. With the aid of this book, you will need less practice to perfect what is one of the most rewarding of all the styles of fishing that are available to today's angler. Good luck and good fishing.

Jan Porter

Opposite: Jan Porter prepares to net a pole-caught carp.

Left: practising what he preaches Jan sets about catching on the pole.

THE JOYS OF POLE FISHING

Poles are nothing new. Several hundred years ago, men were tying lengths of gut with a bait on the end to long pieces of cane and catching fish. With no reels to help them cast, these ancestors of the modern angler were restricted to fishing just a few yards from the bank. Not that that mattered. Britain's rivers and lakes were then so full of fish that it's surprising they had to use bait at all! For a long time, that's how it stayed. Fish, for sport and pot, were taken on what could only be described as forerunners of the modern pole.

Times have changed -- but somehow they haven't. Reels might well have taken angling into new territory, but walk along any canal, river or lake on a Sunday morning and you will see how everything has turned full circle. Poles are once more big business.

Before looking at the reasons for polefishing's popularity, let's get down to basics. What is a pole?

Any length of material – usually carbon or glass-fibre – to which line is attached at one end can be called a pole. There is no reel. They range from the tiniest 1 m 'whips' to lengths of 15 m or more. In fact, some modern – and extremely expensive – poles can now be used at lengths of 18 m.

The whole idea of a pole is to drop a well-presented bait into just the right area without having to cast using a reel. Reels and polefishing do not mix. One does the job of the other, and there is no place for both at the same time. Where, with a 12 or 13-ft rod and a reel, fishing distance is achieved by casting, line being released from the reel, with polefishing distance is achieved through the length of pole used.

If you choose to use a 6-m pole, you fish roughly 6 m

from the bank – often a little more – because that is the restriction imposed by its length. In fact, it is this restriction that puts a lot of people off polefishing when they wonder whether to take it up for the first time. However, by the end of this book I hope you will have discovered that polefishing is an angling method in its own right, enjoyable, rewarding and sometimes the only way to catch fish.

When holding out 11 m of carbon fibre, you may wonder how to land anything you are fortunate enough to hook. One answer is to use 11 m of line as well and simply swing the fish straight out of the water towards you. Even the raw beginner, however, can see that this is highly impractical. Any advantage gained in tackle control would be destroyed with so much line between pole-tip and hook. So what's the answer? It's simple really. With the longest poles, once a fish is hooked, the pole is carefully passed back through the hands in several movements and taken apart. The fish can then be swung to hand or netted. The process is called unshipping and the technique is explained fully later on. Suffice to say here that this is one of the most important parts of polefishing that the beginner has to master and is a process not repeated in any other angling discipline. Decisions on points such as line length are influenced by several factors, but you must make certain that the end of the line coincides with one of the joints. The worst thing of all is to have a length of line that comes half way up one section when the pole is unshipped. The angler has to reach up – or down – for his fish in a clumsy display that can easily be avoided.

Shorter poles – whips – are often fished with an equal length of line, which is much easier to manage. Fishing with the same length of line as the pole or whip is called fishing 'to hand' and is a very fast method much beloved by matchmen, for whom speed is a prime consideration, especially when large numbers of small fish are the quarry.

If polefishing involves learning several new techniques, what is the point of it? Why is polefishing so popular? For the answer to this, it's worth taking a look at its merits over those of more conventional fishing with rod and reel.

First, as no casting weight is required to propel the tackle to the desired distance, very light tackle can be used with poles – much lighter than would be possible with a rod-and-reel set-up over distances of more than a few metres from the bank. Where a pole float taking only a few No.8 shot might be the right choice for a particular swim, a waggler float for rod-and-reel fishing might need three BBs to reach the same spot. If the fish are shy, this can make a considerable difference to your catches. Lighter floats usually mean better, more natural bait presentation, as long as they are heavy enough to combat any wind that might be affecting the water.

Second, many spots which would be very difficult to cast accurately to with rod and reel can be reached with ease with a pole. Try casting a small waggler across to the far side of a canal and you'll soon appreciate the difficulty. With a pole, however, gossamer-light tackle can be carefully pushed right under the trailing branches to the shy fish lying underneath.

Similarly, you can be certain that you are dropping the tackle right into the same spot every time when polefishing. There's much more guesswork involved with rod-and-reel fishing, where you never really know from one cast to the next where exactly you are fishing. With a pole, if you want to fish a little further out or closer to the

Polefishing is now a recognisable method among match and pleasure anglers.

Author Kevin Wilmot swings in a pole-caught roach.

bank, simply add on or remove a section.

Finally, good tackle control is easier with a pole than it is in many cases with a rod and reel, because there is less line between pole-tip and float than between rod-tip and float. The more line you have out, the more line there is to be dragged around by inconsistent flow or wind.

All this isn't to say that there is no place for rod and reel when it comes to floatfishing. It is a mistake to become obsessed with the pole, despite the certain fact that once you've started using one you'll love it! Many anglers do suffer from 'pole-itis' – using the pole at the expense of everything else, even when other methods might be more productive on the day. For the sake of fairness, it is worth pointing out those occasions and situations where polefishing is not recommended or is downright impossible.

The biggest limitation, of course, is distance. When polefishing, the angler is handicapped in that he cannot fish much further out than the length of his pole – even though on many waters this will be ample. These restrictions do not apply in the same way when using a rod and reel with float tackle. Here, the angler can simply put a bigger float on his line, which will give him the extra casting weight to reach the required distance.

Not only distance from the bank, but also distance covered by his tackle in flowing water can limit the pole angler. When polefishing, there is no extra line to be released once the line between pole-tip and float is tight towards the downstream end of the swim. The problem is solved for the rod-and-reel angler by releasing more line from the reel: opening the bale arm and letting line flow from the spool either by allowing the current to pull it out, by moving the rod in an upstream arc, or by pulling it between his fingers.

A second consideration has to be the size of fish expected. Many large fish, including carp well in excess of 10 lb in weight, have been landed on frail pole tackle thanks to shock-absorbing techniques described later. However, line cannot be given to a running fish as it can with rod-and-reel tackle. When a large fish is hooked on rod-and-reel tackle, it can be played using the reel to give line when it runs. When a large fish is hooked on pole tackle, there is no extra line to give it if required, so it has to be played out making use of a special elastic set-up inside the pole tip. Although strong elastic can be rigged so that large fish can be landed if some are expected, such strong elastic is unsuitable for small fish. Here much finer stuff is needed, so should the angler hook something more substantial, his chances of landing it are reduced.

Finally, weather conditions can have quite a bearing on the effectiveness of a pole. A strong wind will tend to blow a long pole around, especially if it is one of the cheaper, less stiff versions. With a float rod being only 12 or 13 ft long, it will be less susceptible to the effects of the elements. However, don't forget that a strong wind can also play havoc with line once it is in the water – and there's much more line in the water when casting with a rod and reel than when fishing in the same place with a pole.

Even with these points in mind, the pole angler often has the edge over his rod-and-reel rival. It is a deadly method for the match angler and England's long-standing ambition to win the world championship using a pole was finally realized in 1991 when they triumphed in Bulgaria, Bob Nudd clinching the individual crown for a second successive year. No longer are English matchmen regarded as second-class citizens when it comes to polefishing. For years they were behind the French, Belgians and Italians, but once anglers realized what polefishing had to offer, top-flight English match anglers worked hard to perfect the techniques. They even refined a lot of them for British fisheries, and now the pole lies alongside more traditional methods as a real fish-catching weapon. Thousands of anglers – match and pleasure alike – have added the pole to their armoury, because undoubtedly there are days when everything will fail to catch – except the pole.

Before embarking on your first tentative steps to perfect polefishing, a word of warning. Carbon-fibre poles are excellent conductors of electricity and several anglers have been killed when their long poles have accidentally touched overhead electricity wires. ALWAYS check before fishing – in front, overhead and behind you – and if you are in any doubt, move swims. They might look like telephone cables, but it's better to be on the safe side. DON'T FISH NEAR CABLES!

Once you've acquired that all-important first pole, try to learn everything you can about this branch of our sport. One thing is certain: once you've grasped the basics of polefishing, you'll want to find out more. Hopefully this book will help you do just that.

CHAPTER ONE

CHOOSING A POLE

Buying that first pole is one of the most important decisions faced by the potential pole angler. There are so many things to be taken into consideration that it can seem an impossible task sorting the wheat from the chaff. Whereas, not so many years ago, there were only a few poles on the market to choose from, now there are hundreds from manufacturers all over the world. It is not the intention to mention too many manufacturers here. Suffice it to say that most pole-manufacturing companies have their good products, their reasonable ones and their sub-standard ones. Let's take a look at the different types available.

As with so many things in life, the angler's prime consideration has to be finance. Not everyone can go out and spend over £1,000 on a new pole, despite the advice of the angling press on what's best for this or that. You get what you pay for, and anyone with the slightest interest in polefishing will know that money buys poles. A lot of money will buy a good pole and a little money won't. It's as simple as that. So the first piece of advice has to be: save up until you can afford a pole you feel happy with. Whether this is £200 or £2,000 depends very much on the angler and his conscience.

Far left: some anglers prefer a very stiff pole.

Below: breakdown of an 11 m pole.

While it might be fine for the unmarried to save well-earned pennies over several months, the married mortgage-payer is often forced to have very different priorities.

Looking first at long poles – 8 m or more – you will get little change from £200, and this, in truth, will not buy you a pole you can feel totally happy with. In fact for a decent 11-m pole – the commonest length on sale – you can expect to pay £400. For this sort of money you will have a pole that you can use adequately in most conditions. Compare it to one costing twice as much and the difference will quickly become apparent. But just how much you spend is your decision. The second-hand tackle columns in *Angling Times* can be a lifesaver. Scan these for bargains and don't be scared to make that phone call – someone else could beat you to it. It's an often-used piece of advice but worth repeating again: buy the longest pole you can afford. Buy an 8-m pole and you will probably soon want a 9-m one. Buy a 9 and you'll soon want a 10 – it's a catch-22 situation and one reason (in addition to the advent of new technology) why poles are appearing in ever-increasing lengths, and are used to great effect at amazing distances by the likes of Bob Nudd.

Assuming you have saved up enough money to buy yourself a decent pole, we now have to look at the other things you need to check before making your purchase, and the first of these is materials. The cheapest poles are made either from glass-fibre or a somewhat dubious material described as 'carbon composite'. This usually means glass-fibre with some sort of strengthening, stiffening agent added. Many companies offer poles in these materials in lengths up to 10 m and some are actually quite good. However, it is unlikely that you will be able to use this sort of pole comfortably in windy conditions, especially in the longer lengths. The pole will feel heavy, floppy and cumbersome, and sag towards the tip.

Likewise, the tip will bounce around for several seconds when the butt is moved. In practical terms this could mean lost fish, the pole's bounce pulling lightly hooked fish off the hook. It is also likely to have a wide diameter at the butt. All this makes for uncomfortable fishing, but it does provide a sound grounding for anyone trying their hand at polefishing for the first time

– just don't expect to be putting in world championship performances when you take it out to the riverbank.

The newcomer to polefishing might not notice these qualities in a 'cheap' pole, thinking all poles behave in a similar fashion. All that changes when he tries one made out of carbon fibre. As with rods, the advent of carbon brought an enormous improvement in the poles that were commercially available. Poles suddenly became usable by anglers other than those built like brick outhouses. The improvement is still going on today. The first carbon poles, although a vast improvement on their glass-fibre predecessors, were heavy, sloppy and cumbersome by today's standards. What you don't know you don't miss, however, and would-be pole anglers thought they'd struck gold. Now, all sorts of techniques and materials are employed to make further improvements in weight, diameter and rigidity. Materials such as kevlar, lithium and amorphous are used in the manufacturing process, combined with the carbon fibre in elaborate 'weaves' running the length of the pole from butt to tip. The best poles have successfully achieved a near-perfect combination of these three essential criteria – little weight, little diameter and much rigidity.

I've already stated that most reasonable poles that are in the shops come at a basic length of 11 m, and this is the length the would-be pole angler should endeavour to afford. Even the most proficient of pole anglers would probably admit that they rarely use their pride and joys at lengths beyond this. It coincides with the far shelf on the majority of canals and gets them well out into rivers and lakes.

Extensions of 1 or 1½ metres are usually available to add to the butt section of these poles should a longer one be required – but again, they can cost a lot of money if the pole is to retain its good qualities. If you're worried that 11 m might not be long enough, pace it out in the back garden. You'll realize that 11 m will be perfectly adequate for most polefishing situations. An 11-m pole costing a lot of money will even feel uncomfortable at first to the angler used to wielding 13-ft float rods. It's a question of technique and the familiarity that comes with regular use. Techniques for holding a long pole in comfort are described fully later on.

Joints

The way in which each section of a long pole joins together might not seem very important to the beginner, but the angler who has been polefishing for some time knows that good joints can make or break a pole – literally. Pole joints come in three types – telescopic, put-in and put-over. Telescopic joints are used exclusively for short whips and highly specialized long poles, and should not be considered by the angler buying his first long pole. The two important ones are put-in and put-over. So what's the difference? Quite simply, with poles that have put-in joints, the sections nearer the pole-tip fit inside those nearer the butt. With poles that have put-over joints, the sections nearer the pole-tip fit outside (or over) those nearer the butt.

In practice, the beginner to polefishing will notice little difference between the two types. However, during recent years there has been a definite trend among good pole anglers towards poles with put-over joints. This type of pole, it is said, is better to use because put-over joints are easier to locate than put-ins. Furthermore, all pole joints wear, but when put-over joints wear, all that happens is that the section nearer the butt pushes further inside the next section, nearer the tip. When put-in joints wear, eventually the male joint on the section nearer the tip will slide completely through the female joint on the next section nearer the butt. In addition to all this, poles with put-over joints tend to be slimmer overall than their put-in counterparts, and lighter too. Perhaps the only aspect on which put-in poles are

Below left: put -in joints are like this.

Below right: put-over joints are like this.

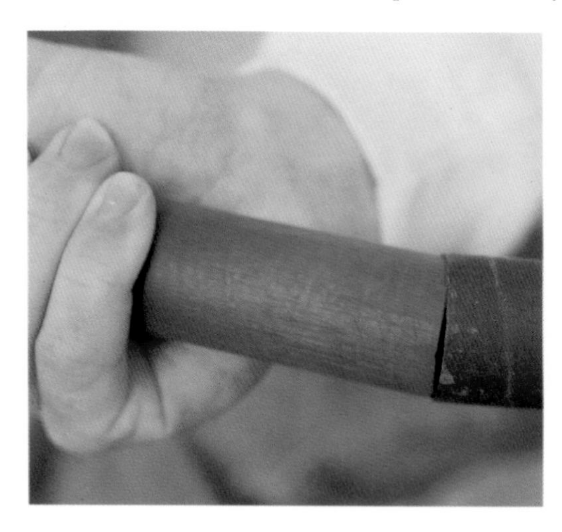

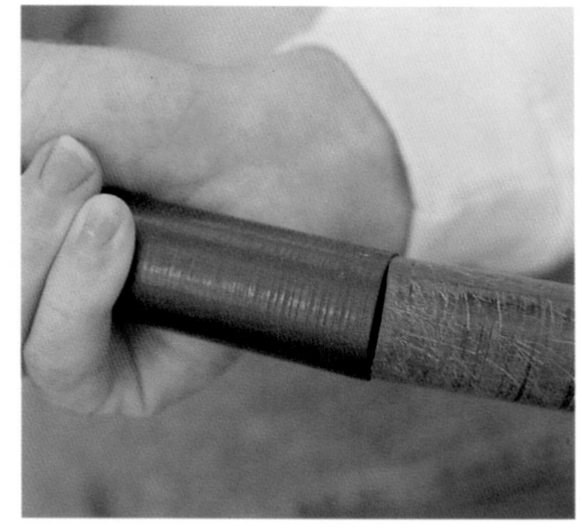

World champion Bob Nudd has been responsible for many British pole techniques.

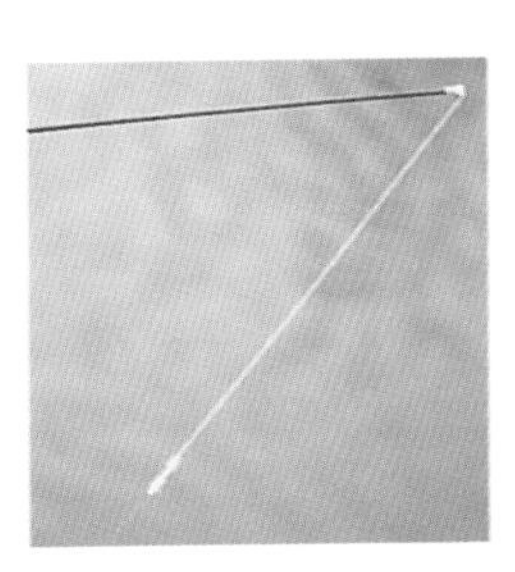

Pole tip sections have to be cut back to take elastic.

superior is rigidity. Some of the stiffest, sturdiest poles ever made have put-in joints, and anglers who visit fish-packed countries like Ireland and Denmark often take this sort of pole with them.

No poles have put-over joints only. In fact, often the top two or top three sections are telescopic, while sometimes the top section pushes inside the next. Be careful with poles whose top three sections are telescopic. This might pose problems when a very short length of line is required between pole-tip and hook – for pushing under the branches of a far-side tree on a shallow canal, for example. With the top three sections being at least 2 m long in total, that is the shortest length of line than be used comfortably and a shorter line might be required. Poles whose top two sections are telescopic, or fully take-apart poles, are better.

Spares

Another important point to look into when buying a new pole is the availability of spare parts. There are few pole anglers who have not at some time or other broken a section or watched one disappear under the water surface. You need to know that replacement sections are available without too long a wait, and at a fair price, too. On the subject of spares, check also whether your pole comes just as it is, or whether extra top sections are included in the price. It is certainly useful to have more than one top-three pole-tip as different elastic set-ups can be fitted through each one. Many pole anglers like several different rigs set up beside them while fishing. Having more than one top part certainly saves time and energy in this department. Several manufacturers sensibly provide a spare top-three section with their poles, while some tackle dealers will also provide a spare top-three for little extra cost.

Tip sections

Take a close look at the pole's tip section before buying. The chances are it will be hollow and quite long. This is the most common type of tip section and is designed to be cut back so an internal shock-absorbing set-up can be fitted. The tip sections on some poles are stiffer than those on others. The softest tip sections are usually longer and have to be cut back considerably more than the other type to allow elastic to be fitted so that the tip does not bend too much when a fish is hooked, reducing the effect of the elastic as it rubs against the inside of the tip section. A third type of tip on a long pole is known as a flick-tip and is a length of fine, tapering and solid carbon spliced into the hollow tip. This is not designed to house elastic – as it is solid, elastic cannot be fitted inside – but acts as a shock absorber by itself. Some accomplished pole anglers prefer this flick-tip set-up for catching large numbers of small fish quickly, but with the lack of elastic to help with playing larger fish, it is a dangerous technique if anything at all substantial is likely to be hooked. Your chances of landing it are minimal.

Action

In today's technologically advanced world of polefishing, it is possible to buy poles with just about any action you want. And as the pole angler becomes more proficient, he will realize that it is not always the stiffest poles that are best. For example, anglers who concentrate most of their attentions on canals with light tackle and long poles, might place lightness at the top of their list of priorities. The fact that the lightest poles usually lose out slightly in the rigidity stakes does not bother them. However, the river angler is likely to place rigidity higher on the list than lightness. So decide what sort of action you want before making that all-important purchase.

Whips

Similar criteria to the above can be laid out when buying a whip, which is really a shorter pole, often all telescopic or part telescopic and part take-apart. Telescopic whips are designed for fishing with a length of line that is the same as the length of the whip. It is fishing at its simplest – the tackle is swung out to the desired fishing spot, and the fish are swung back in again! It sounds easy, but there are considerations to be borne in mind when deciding whether or not to use a whip. The action of the wind on the water, for example, can severely reduce the whip's effectiveness, blowing tackle and line all over the place. A long pole and shorter line, unshipping to catch, allows better tackle control. However, there is no doubt that a whip fished effectively can be much faster than conventional polefishing. All-telescopic whips are available in a wide range of lengths from 1 to 10 m although the most common lengths in use on British waters are 3, 4 and 5 m. Canal anglers will tell you that you need 2-m whips, while river anglers will always carry whips of 6 m and perhaps 7 m. However, for your first purchase, buy a whip of 4 or 5 m. On most venues between 4 and 8 ft deep, a 5-m whip will allow you to cast out far enough to find the fish.

Nine times out of ten, whips are used with flick-tips, in order to catch large numbers of small fish quickly. An elastic set-up with a stiffish tip section would result in a lot of 'bumped' fish, so whip anglers usually prefer a flick-tip, resorting to chance should a big fish come along to take the bait. It is quite amazing how large fish can be landed on a whip – sometimes they're in the net before they have realized they've even been hooked! The only time anglers should consider using an elastic set-up when whip fishing is for highly specialized requirements such as fishing for carp in lakes where large numbers of fish to 3 lb are taken close to the bank. These fish can be landed successfully as long as some sort of shock absorber is used to control that first run of the hooked fish.

A few years ago, it was true to say that the only whips to consider in terms of action and lightness were all-telescopic ones. Now, however, the angler is spoilt for choice and it is possible to buy one whip that can be used in several different lengths. Manufacturers have achieved this by a combination of telescopic and take-apart sections, and there are now many excellent whips of this type available. Most have a top 3 or 4 m that are telescopic, followed by several add-on sections to extend the length. There are several advantages in this. The whip can be used simply for to-hand fishing as normal. It can be used with a short length of line corresponding just to the telescopic section, with extra sections added on to gain extra length while still retaining a good degree of tackle control in a wind. And the angler can follow the fish, adding on a section if the fish decide to move further away from the bank as the session progresses. As you can see, a part take-apart and part telescopic whip serves several purposes and is an excellent buy.

Whip action can be split into two types: those which are designed purely for catching large numbers of small-to-medium fish (½ oz to 6 oz), and those for larger fish. The first type are quite stiff through the flick-tip or the second section, after which they bend. It is this tip part that acts as the shock absorber when a fish is hooked, to prevent the hook pulling from its mouth. Once hooked, however, the fish should be removed from the water as quickly as possible, and this is where the stiffer sections of the whip do their job. Shorter whips (up to 4 m) are usually of this action. However, when longer whips are used, the action is much softer. Much more of the whip bends and they often have a hollow, flexible tip section. These whips bend in a gradual curve, aiding the casting of light floats and enabling large fish to be played successfully to the net. They can be highly effective in deep-water swims, or on rivers where the flow of the water requires more line to allow the float to travel the full length of the swim. Reasonable whips can cost anything from £40 to £200. If you can afford just one, go for a part telescopic and part take-apart model of around 5 or 6 m in length.

Fishing the whip is fast and fun.

CHAPTER TWO

ELASTICS

Once you have bought a new pole, you'll be itching to get to the bank of your favourite river or lake to put it through its paces, but first there are several important things you have to do at home. In fact, half the fun of polefishing is the preparation involved – it makes that first pole-caught fish something special!

Before you even start work fitting elastic and making rigs, check the pole very carefully. It's unlikely that you will have been sold a faulty one, but a few will always slip through the net and it is worth examining every section carefully for cracks or splits, especially around the joints. Only when you are satisfied that your pole is in first-class condition should you start to work on it. If you feel inclined – and it's certainly a good idea – treat each joint with the special protective solution that is now available, called Jointsave. This adds strength to each joint, prolongs the life of your pole, and reduces wear, which shows in untreated poles in the form of black carbon 'dust' on the affected section. This is especially noticeable in the wet. You should also insure your pole before using it. With tackle thefts on the increase, it's a foolish angler who does not make plans for such an eventuality. As your pole is likely to be the most expensive item of kit in your collection, that should go at the top of the list.

Let us assume that the pole is fine, it's been insured, and you have taken the wise step of buying an extra top-section kit to go with the two supplied with the

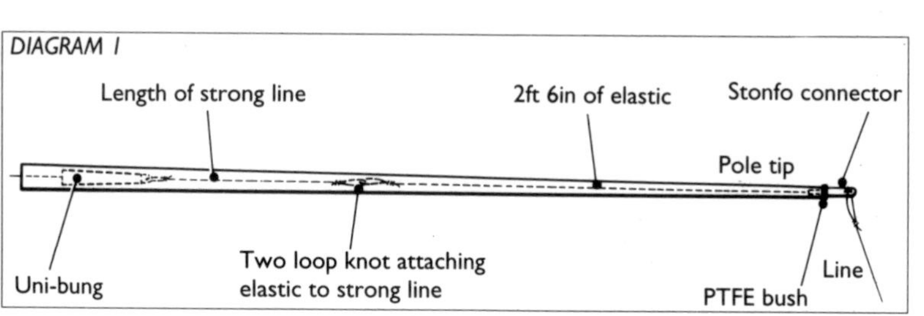

A typical pole-tip elastic set-up. This one includes a length of strong line so exactly 2ft 6in of elastic can be used.

pole. Your next job is to fit them with elastic. The use of elastic is an alien concept to newcomers to polefishing. However, it is an extremely important fish-catching aid. When using a rod and reel, once a fish is hooked the angler simply reels in and swings the fish to hand or nets it in the usual way. If it's a big fish, he can let it run if required, either by setting the reel's clutch so that the fish pulls line from the spool, or by backwinding – turning the reel's handle backwards – to give fish line. With a pole, neither of these two things can be done – there is no more line apart from that between pole-tip and hook. The answer is to incorporate a length of elastic inside the top part of the pole. It is this elastic that does one part of the job of a reel. It doesn't magically produce extra line so a fish can run and still be landed, but it extends when a fish is hooked. If the fish is small, it might only be pulled 1 to 2 in before retracting back inside the pole to allow the fish to be landed. However, when the fish is big, it really does its work. The elastic is pulled out from the pole-tip, increasing in tension as it does so and eventually tiring the fish, which can then be landed in the normal way. It is an extremely effective way of landing large fish – neat, tidy and reliable as long as the elastic is checked on a regular basis.

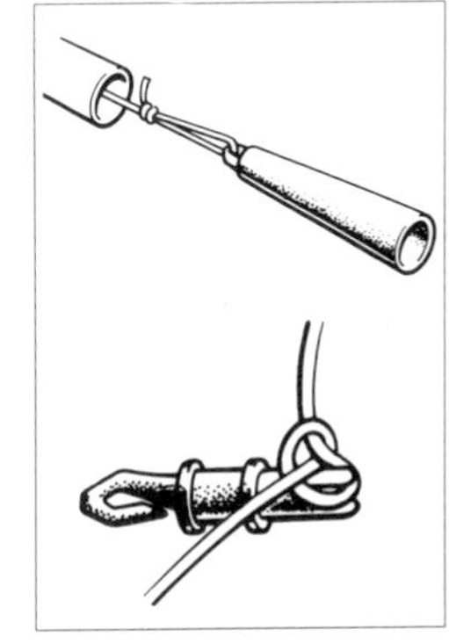

The Uni-bung (top) and Stonfo Connector: useful items for the pole angler.

Types and strenghts

There are several types of elastic designed for polefishing – all thin, circular and able to stretch a long length. It is obvious that one size of elastic will not suffice for every situation the pole angler is likely to encounter. That's why it comes in many different strengths and thicknesses, which can be used for different circumstances. Catching small fish along the far shelf of a canal, for example, should require a fine elastic, while larger fish on rivers can be handled with a thicker one. The strongest elastic, meanwhile, is designed for large species. Large fish would soon pull a length of fine elastic to its limit and the angler's chance of landing it would be minimal; using thick elastic for small fish will undoubtedly lead to a lot of 'bumped' fish, the strike being too powerful and pulling the hook through the fish's mouth. But still there are problems.

What about times when most fish will be small, but

Modern elastic comes in different colours as well as different strengths.

Far right: the real test of a pole comes when a big fish is hooked.

the occasional larger one can be expected? Choice of elastic is one of the skills of the pole angler, but with more than half-a-dozen sizes available, there is usually one to suit your needs. You can always change during a session. Now you can see the importance of several top sections!

Britain's two most popular elastics are those under the brand names of Slip and Zim. Others are available that should meet your requirements equally well – check which are stocked by your local dealer. Both of these elastics are excellent, but you will notice that Slip elastic is colour-coded for easy identification. That is a great advantage to the pole angler when it comes to selecting elastic before starting to fish. Pole elastics are coded according to thickness and breaking strain. Don't worry too much about breaking strain – it is merely a guide and only ever comes into play when the elastic 'bottoms out' (reaches the limit of its stretch). Your choice of strength and length of elastic should by determined by three factors: the size of fish you will be catching, the depth of the water, and the size of your float.

Consult the table as a guide, but remember that the best anglers are prepared to change according to what's happening in front of them. The best way of finding the right elastic on your chosen venue is to experiment with different elastics, different lengths and different tensions. An elastic which might work on one venue may result in bumped fish on another, similar venue. Fish like

Zim	Slip	Size of fish	Size of float	Depth of water	No of sections	Diameter	Species
1	Purple	Up to 8 oz	Up to 0.7 gm	Up to 4 ft	1	0.58 mm	Roach, gudgeon
2	Red	Up to 1 lb	Up to 1 gm	Up to 8 ft	1	0.67 mm	Roach, skimmers
3	Green	Up to 2 lb	Up to 1.5 gm	Up to 8 ft	1 or 2	0.75 mm	Roach, bream
4	Orange	Up to 3 lb	Up to 2.5 gm	Up to 12 ft	1 or 2	0.85 mm	Roach, bream
5	Blue	Up to 4 lb	Up to 3 gm	Up to 12 ft	2	0.91 mm	Bream, chub
6	Yellow	Up to 5 lb	Up to 4 gm	Up to 15 ft	2	1.06 mm	Carp, barbel
7	-	Up to 6 lb	Up to 5 gm	Up to 18 ft	2	1.18 mm	Carp, eels
8	Grey	Up to 8 lb	Up to 6 gm	Up to 20 ft	2	1.37 mm	Carp, eels

Above: a table showing elastic guidelines.

skimmer bream have soft mouths, and if your elastic is not exactly right, you will lose more than you catch. In truth, all species can prove difficult to hook unless the right pole elastic and tension is used. The well-prepared angler will ensure that he has several different set-ups, then one can be changed in seconds for another. This can prove costly in the first instance, but will eventually pay dividends.

Fitting elastic

Of course, if pole elastic is to do its job effectively and reliably, it has to be fitted properly – and there are specific tools for the job. It is most important that the elastic flows smoothly from the pole-tip. An elastic that flows in a series of awkward jerks is a recipe for disaster – lost fish at best, snapped elastic and lost tackle at worst. The main problem lies at the tip of the pole. Even a carefully cut pole-tip, smoothed with fine sandpaper, will cause abrasion and damage elastic, so something has to be fitted into the tip to provide a friction-free surface over which the elastic can glide smoothly

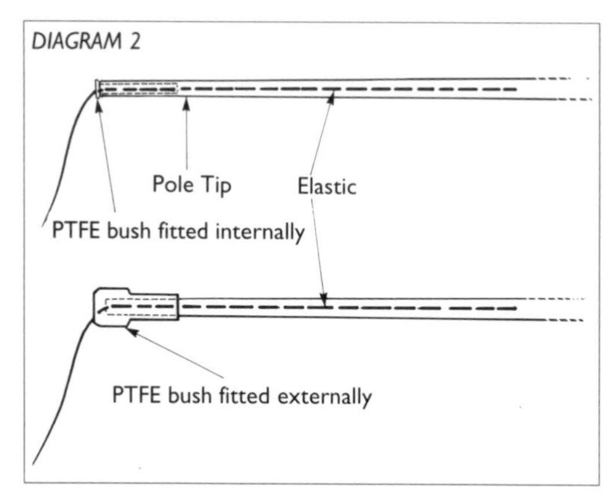

Internal (top) and external bushes. Internal are best.

without damage. The answer is a PTFE bush. PTFE is an almost friction-free material that is used in space rockets among other things, and it is the answer to a pole-angler's prayers. A correctly fitted PTFE bush will give years of trouble-free service, although the elastic will need changing from time to time.

PTFE bushes are small, neat and can be fitted internally or externally, depending on the diameter of the hollow pole-tip and how much is cut off. Internal bushes are generally regarded as preferable because there is no way the elastic can scrape against the rough tip of the pole. This can happen, however, with a badly fitted external bush – so take care. External bushes used to be popular because, as none of the bush is inside the pole-tip, very little had to be cut off the pole-tip, reducing the length of the pole by only a few inches. Now, tiny 'micro-tips' are available, which can still be fitted internally but without having to lose much from the pole's length.

With the PTFE bush at the very tip of the pole, what about the other end of the elastic? It will have to be secured in some way, and again there are items tailor-made for the job. Elastic securing bungs come in several shapes and sizes, and it's largely a matter of personal choice. For elastic that is to be fitted into the wider, second section, a bung which can be cut to fit neatly inside is ideal. If this bung has the facility to allow the tension of the elastic to be changed quickly and easily without breaking it and starting again, so much the better. A bung that fits inside the pole is necessary if the next section down fits inside the section with the bung, as on put-over poles. If the next section fits outside the bung section – a put-in pole – then a different kind of

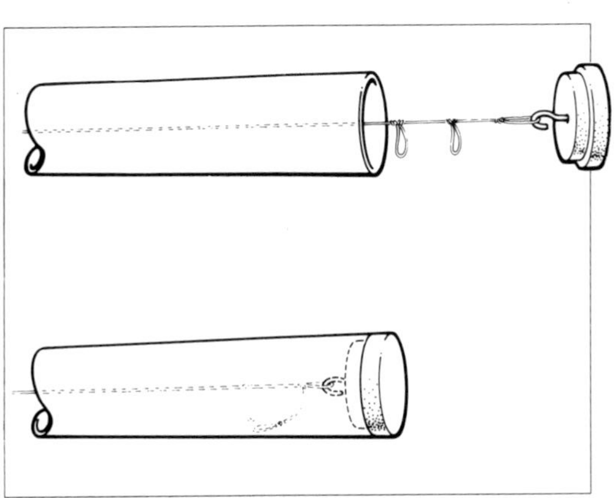

Elastic tension can be altered quickly by tying small loops at 3-in intervals.

Far right, six easy steps to fitting pole elastic.

bung can be used, fitting neatly over the end of the joint. The put-over pole bung can be used with both types of section.

As well as bung and bush, you will need some means of joining the elastic to your line. An Italian device called a Stonfo Connector is great for the job, but there are other ways of doing it which are just as effective and not as bulky. The Stonfo is a simple, plastic device with a hook at one end, over which a loop in the line slides. It is secured by a plastic sleeve. The end of the elastic is tied to the other end of the connector and everything is neat, tidy and secure.

Pole-elastic lubricant is a must for the pole angler. Regular treatments with this helps the elastic to flow more smoothly through the pole-tip sections, repelling water and prolonging the life of the elastic. Use it after fitting and tightening all knots, and before every fishing session. Several drops should be poured into the tip sections.

A good tackle dealer will often fit elastic into your pole-tip sections if you ask him nicely, but it is a useful ploy to learn how to do this yourself. The things you will need are: PTFE bush, tip connector, bung, elastic, elastic threader, pole-tip section or top two sections, wet-and-dry paper, small scissors and hacksaw blade.

PTFE bushes come in many shapes, colours and sizes.

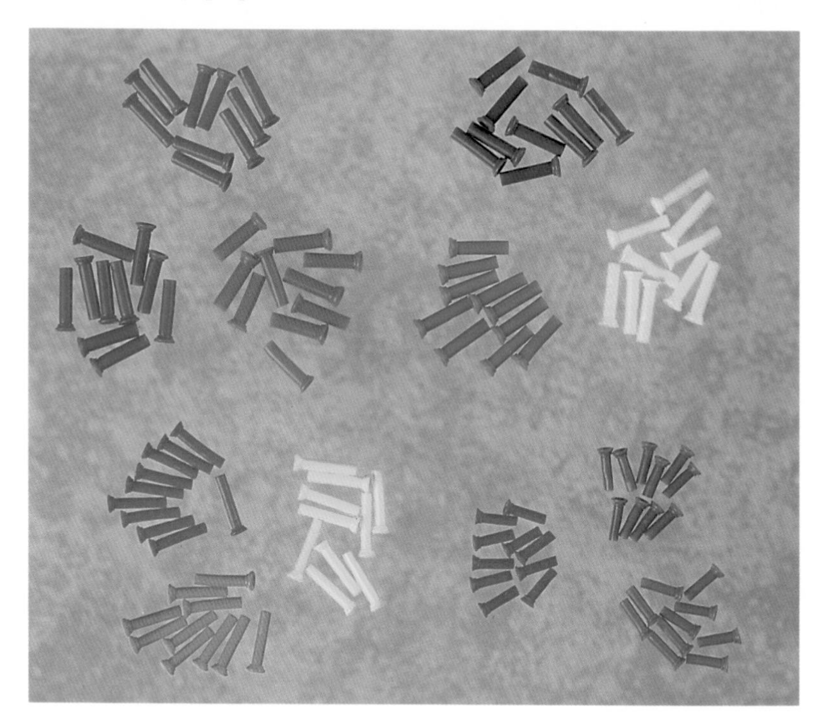

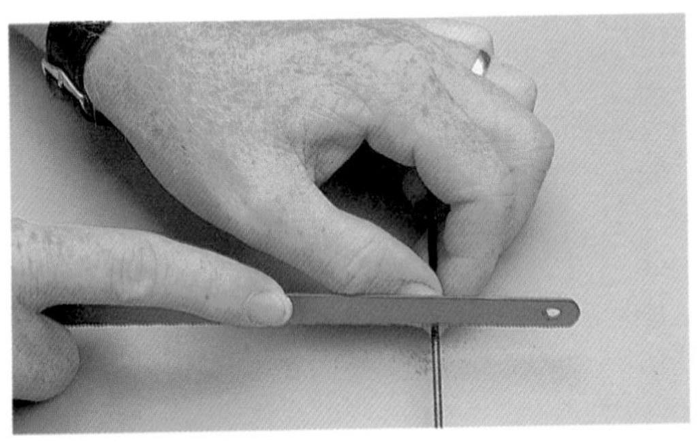

STEP 1

Check whether your chosen PTFE bush – it should allow the elastic to pass through with only a tiny space all round – fits inside the pole-tip, or outside if you want to use an external bush. The chances are that it won't, so use a hacksaw blade to saw carefully through the tip of the pole a few inches from the end. Score all the way round with the blade before sawing through to prevent splinters shearing away.

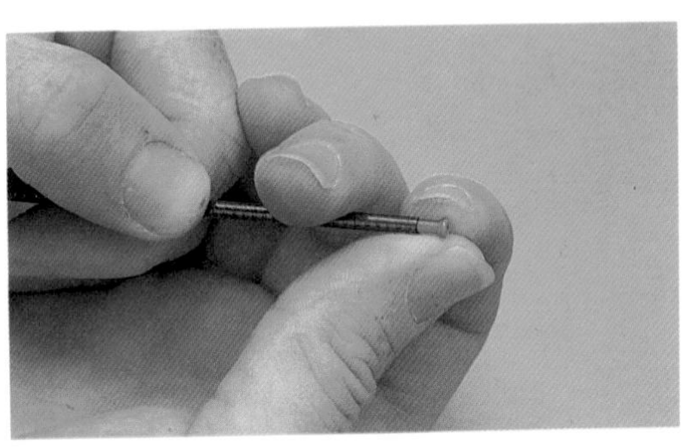

STEP 2

Try the bush for size again. If it fits tightly, push it in or over the tip. If it doesn't, cut a little more off – 1 in at a time is about right – until the bush fits tightly. Now remove the bush and sand the tip edge smooth with wet-and-dry paper. Fit the bush for a last time. Carefully glue it in place if you want to, but if you have cut the pole tip back correctly, you shouldn't need to do this.

STEP 3

Take your chosen bung and, assuming you want elastic through the top two sections of your pole, ensure it fits into the butt end of the second section. If you are using a Uni-bung, it should be gently scored by turning it against the bottom of the second section. Then cut and remove the unwanted part of the bung without cutting through the inner nylon tag. Sand the cut edge smooth.

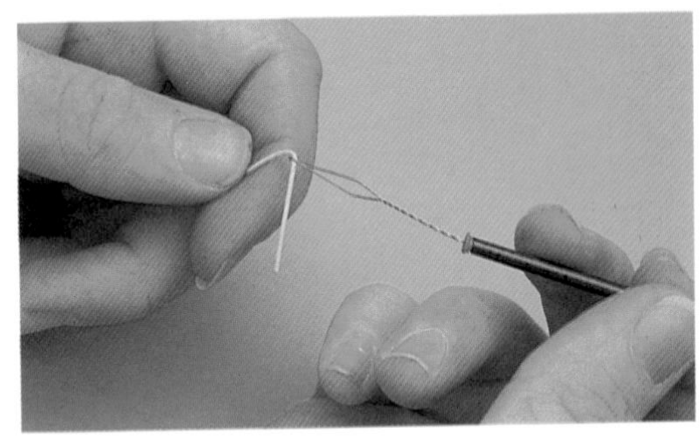

STEP 4

Attach the elastic to the special threader – all tackle shops sell them – and push threader and elastic through from the tip sections. Once it's through, attach the tip connector by using at least two overhand knots, tightening each carefully so there is no chance of the elastic slipping.

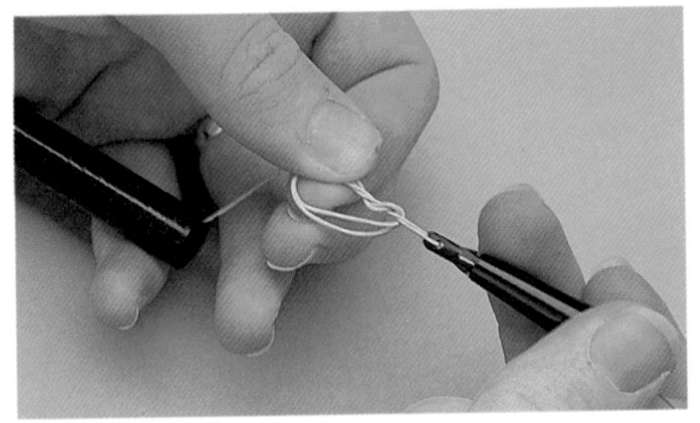

STEP 5

Once the elastic has been threaded and the tip connector tied and pulled against the bush, take the other end and, after removing the threader, pull it to the tension you require. Trim off the excess and thread the end of the elastic through the hole in the bung. Tie to the bung using a well-tightened single overhand loop. Some bungs have a hook. Here, tie a loop and hook it over.

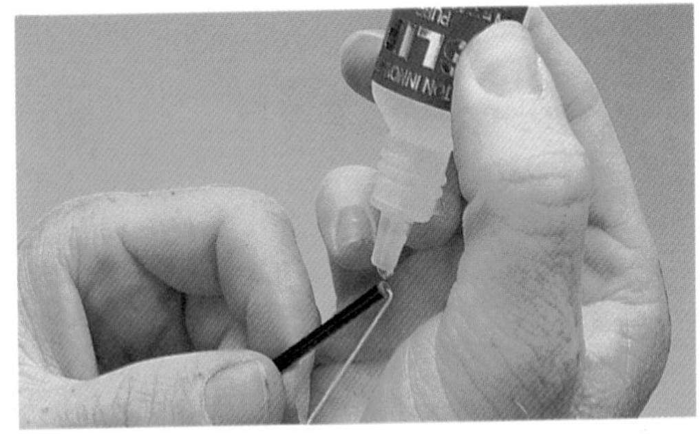

STEP 6

Test the elastic for tension, adjusting it at the bung end if necessary, and treat it with pole-elastic lubricant to ensure that it flows smoothly through the tip. You can make further adjustments on the bankside.

Length of elastic

Anglers with poles whose top section is quite long often use elastic through the top section only, and in the small sizes of elastic it's unlikely that you will need any more than around 18 in of fine elastic. However, a different type of bung is required here. The best tip-section bungs are made in Italy by Stonfo and are available in 10 different diameters from 2.8 mm to 12.4 mm. Once a loop has been tied in the end of the elastic, it is attached to a plug of the correct size, which then fits on to the end of the tip section.

For many polefishing situations, elastic through one section will be enough. With a tip section of at least 12 in long, there will be enough elastic to handle fish of 2 or 3 lb as long as you are careful. This is fine for small-to-medium sized fish, but what about larger fish where stronger, thicker elastic is required? In this case a longer length of elastic is needed as there would not be enough of a shock absorber in a short length of strong elastic.

On waters where fish like chub and carp may be encountered, elastic through the top two sections is best. Some top anglers are so adamant about the length of elastic they want that they measure it out to their chosen length disregarding the length of the top two sections of their pole. The elastic is then tied using the two-loop knot to a length of strong line long enough to allow a bung to be removed from the butt of the second section.

Getting the tension right is something that comes with trial and error. The best advice is to fit the elastic so it only just slides back into the pole when pulled from the tip end. The chances are this will be too slack when it comes to fishing, but better too slack than too tight. It's easy to cut the elastic at the bung end, tie another loop and replace the bung to make everything tighter, but it's much more difficult to slacken elastic that's too tight. One way is to use a plug with a hook. Then you can tie three loops in the end of the elastic at 3-in intervals, instead of one loop, and hook over whichever loop makes the elastic work best. Another way is to use a special sort of bung, whose diameter can be adjusted to allow it to be fitted further up or down the second section. There are also special elastic tensioners available, which can be used to tighten the elastic, or slacken it again afterwards. All these are excellent ways to get your elastic just right – it should not be hanging loose from the pole-tip, but should not be too tight either. It should do its job on all sizes of fish, pulling out when the fish is hooked, then coming into play if required as the fish is brought towards the net.

If you have just one top section, or the top two sections, for elastic, you can still change elastic on the riverbank by preparing the right length at home, with a connector tied to one end but nothing at the other. Wrap it around a pole-rig winder and store it in your tackle box. Should you want to change, you can then simply thread it through from the tip with an elastic threader, and attach a bung to the other end.

Top match angler, Bob Nudd, has come up with an innovative way of attaching elastic at the tip section, which does away with the need for a Stonfo connector. It is brilliant for fine elastic and fine tip sections, where a Stonfo connector can be an obtrusive hindrance on otherwise delicate tackle. It's simple to do:

1 Slide a ¼ in length of narrow, stiff tubing over the tip end of the elastic (Bob uses a tiny PTFE bush with the wide end cut off – this gives him the exact amount of stiffness he wants).

2 Tie a single overhand loop in the end of the elastic and then cut the loop close, so you are left with three ends. Cut the ends short so they are each less than a ¼ in long.

3 Now take the end of your pole line and tie a double overhand loop in it of around 1½ in. Tie another, much smaller loop in the end of this larger loop.

4 Pull the line through this large loop and slip your new loop over the elastic between the three short ends and the short length of tubing.

5 Tighten behind the short ends by pulling on the main pole line, ensuring that the loop slips over the knots in the line.

6 Now slide the short length of stiff tubing over the three ends and the tightened line and everything is ready. To remove, simply slide the tubing back and pull on the short loop. It really works!

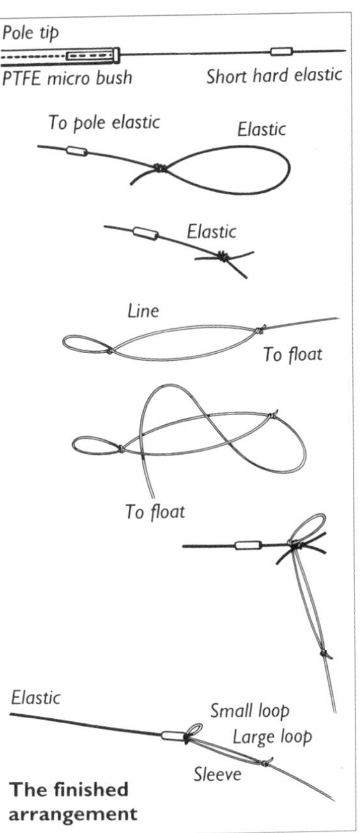

Fitting elastic to line the Bob Nudd way.

CHAPTER THREE

TYPES OF FLOATS

No pole angler will get very far without floats. Not only do floats serve their purpose as indicators of a bite, they also suspend the bait at the required depth and help the angler control his end tackle. However, step into any tackle shop and you will probably be totally confused by the hundreds – sometimes thousands – of floats on display. So what makes a good pole float, or a bad one, for that matter?

Before answering that question, it is worth looking at the requirements of a float for polefishing. First is its weight-carrying capacity. Here lies the main difference between floats for polefishing and those for rod-and-reel

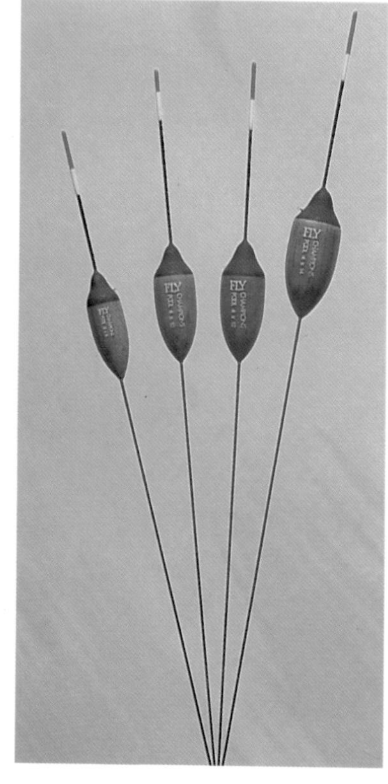

Right: three bristle materials (from left): nylon, wire and cane.

Far right: floats with wire bristles are becoming more and more popular.

Carry duplicates of your favourite floats.

fishing. Floats for rod-and-reel fishing need to serve several different functions but one of their most important requirements is to have the potential to carry enough weight to allow the angler to cast to the required distance without the float sinking out of sight beneath the surface once it has landed. The pole angler does not have such worries. No casting is required for him. Put in the simplest terms, he lowers the tackle on to the water. The weight required in a waggler or stick float with running line is superfluous when polefishing – which immediately highlights one of polefishing's strongest advantages over other forms of fishing.

As pole floats don't have to be cast, they are lighter than floats for other forms of fishing. In most cases, this means that they are more delicate and more sensitive as well. A delicate float, carefully shotted, will entice more bites from a shoal of fickle fish than a heavier float, which has to take more weight in order to be cast to the right place. A pole float can be lowered on to the surface of a shallow canal with almost imperceptible disturbance, completely unnoticed by the fish beneath – imagine a heavy waggler landing in the same place.

And delicacy means sensitivity. The tiny bristle on the top of most pole floats takes only a tiny amount of effort on the part of the fish to pull beneath the surface. The fish feels no resistance and is hooked by the angler on the bank. Floats taking more weight are more likely to be felt by the fish, and the bait dropped before the strike can be made. This is especially important on stillwaters and canals, where a fish has time to inspect a bait, sucking and blowing at it and even taking it into its mouth before any indication is apparent on the float tip. On moving water it's not so important – if a fish doesn't take the bait as it drifts past its nose, it will miss out. So, pole floats are usually lighter than their rod-and-reel counterparts for fishing the same distance from the bank. They're also smaller, and this can be important in clear water like that sometimes found in canals and on many venues in winter. A small float is less likely to be noticed than a large one.

Materials

Just as in floats for rod-and-reel fishing, floats for polefishing come in many shapes and sizes, and the beginner can easily become confused by the vast array available. It's a sad fact that many floats – pole floats included – are designed to catch more anglers than fish, and despite what some pole float brochures would have you believe, you need only a few patterns to see you through most situations. Most pole floats are constructed with a bristle, a body and a stem. They are attached to the line by passing it through a tiny wire eye fixed near the top of the body and through one, two or even three short lengths of narrow rubber sleeve, which slide on to the float stem. The wire eye is a much better attachment than wide, obtrusive float rubbers like those used on stick floats but they won't stand up to the rigours of rod and reels with their continual casting and retrieving. However, for pole floats, they're perfect.

You might wonder why pole floats are attached at the top and bottom, not only at the bottom end like wagglers. In truth, of course, there are times when it pays to use bottom-end-only floats when polefishing, especially when fishing 'to-hand' with a whip, but generally speaking, top-and-bottom floats are preferable. This is because near-perfect control is possible with a pole. Bottom-end floats are used by rod-and-reel anglers because there is a need to sink the line out of the way of the wind between rod tip and float. With a much shorter amount of line between pole tip and float, the effects of the wind are much reduced, so top-and-bottom floats can be used that can be controlled much more easily and are more sensitive than bottom-end only floats. Even in windy conditions, top-and-bottom floats can be controlled when the angler fixes a small shot a few inches above the float – it's called a backshot – to sink a little of the line, which would otherwise be blown around by the wind, affecting the float and ruining the delicate presentation of the bait.

Bristles

The bristles on many pole floats are all part and parcel of their sensitivity, aiding the bite-detection process by all but eliminating any buoyancy at the tip of the float. A fish merely has to breathe on a bait for it to show on a properly-shotted pole-float bristle. The most popular bristle material is nylon, probably because it's the easiest to work with. A small hole is made by the manufacturer in the top of the float body and the bristle is pushed into it. The best pole floats have between ¼ and ½ in of bristle actually in the body, and around 1 in protruding as the bite detector. Often no glue is used to attach the bristle to the float body, with the manufacturers claiming that the bristle can be changed quickly for another one of a different colour if the reflection on the water changes – when the surface goes from calm to ripples, for example. This is not the perfect solution, however, as water tends to seep inside the gap between bristle and float body and affect the setting of the float. What was a perfectly-shotted pole float at the start of a session disappears from view beneath the surface an hour later. For this reason, many anglers glue their bristles in place, changing its colour if they need to by using a quick-drying fluorescent paint (orange or yellow) or indelible felt-tip pen (black).

Nylon bristles, though not buoyant, are not heavy either and a float can be shotted quite easily so just a

Right: an ideal stillwater float with body shaped roughly like a pear.

Far right: far side canal 'dibbers'.

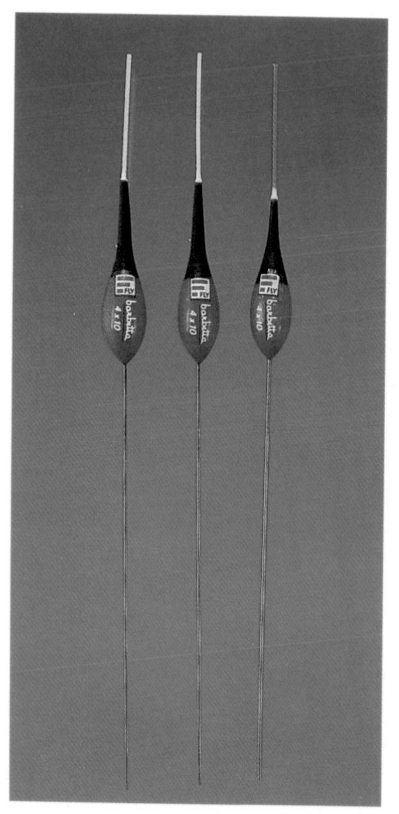

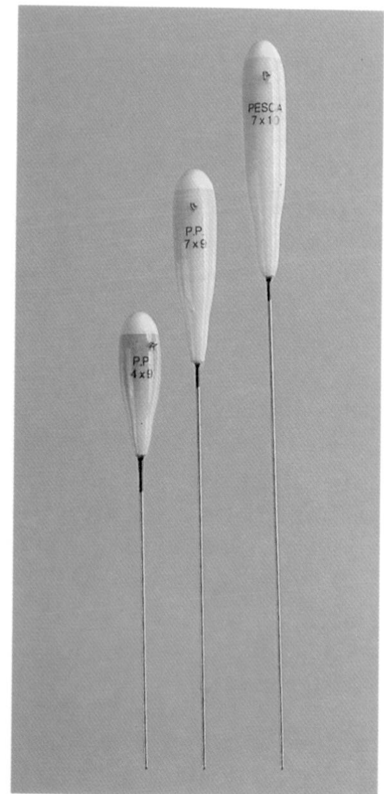

part of the bristle is showing. They come in various thicknesses, which is a good thing as some of the smaller floats have ridiculously fine bristles that just cannot be seen at distances beyond, say, nine metres. Many anglers substitute thicker bristles for these fine ones, or give the fine ones a coat or two of fluorescent paint as an aid to visibility. These thicker bristles are just as sensitive as thinner ones and can actually be shotted so just the very tip is visible above the surface.

Another bristle material much used in the manufacture of pole floats is cane. This material is an excellent choice when a float is required that registers bites as the bait falls through the last part of the water. Good canal anglers use cane bristles when fishing for gudgeon, weighting the pole float with its 'bulk' – most of the float's weight-carrying capacity – around 8 in from the hook and just one or two small shot between this and the hook. These shot are usually No. 8s, and as each one settles, the cane tip on the float settles a little more.

A few trial drops of the tackle soon familiarizes the angler with the behaviour of his float. Gudgeon – and other species – have a habit of coming up a few inches off the bottom as they gain in confidence. Instead of shallowing up and missing out on those fish still on the bottom, the angler has the perfect float. If a fish intercepts the bait as it is falling, once the bulk has settled, it is easily seen on the float by the failure of the cane tip to settle properly because the fish has prevented the bottom 'dropper' shot from settling. Setting a pole with a nylon bristle in this way is not so easy.

The final bristle material is one that is becoming more and more popular with top match anglers after losing popularity for many years. Floats with wire bristles used to be employed all the time by anglers on the Continent – especially in France and Belgium, where polefishing techniques were perfected long before British anglers started realizing its advantages. Now, anglers of the calibre of Bob Nudd and Dave Berrow use wire bristles for much of their polefishing. The great advantage of a wire bristle is its sensitivity – drop a wire bristle into water and it sinks like a stone. Once a float with a wire

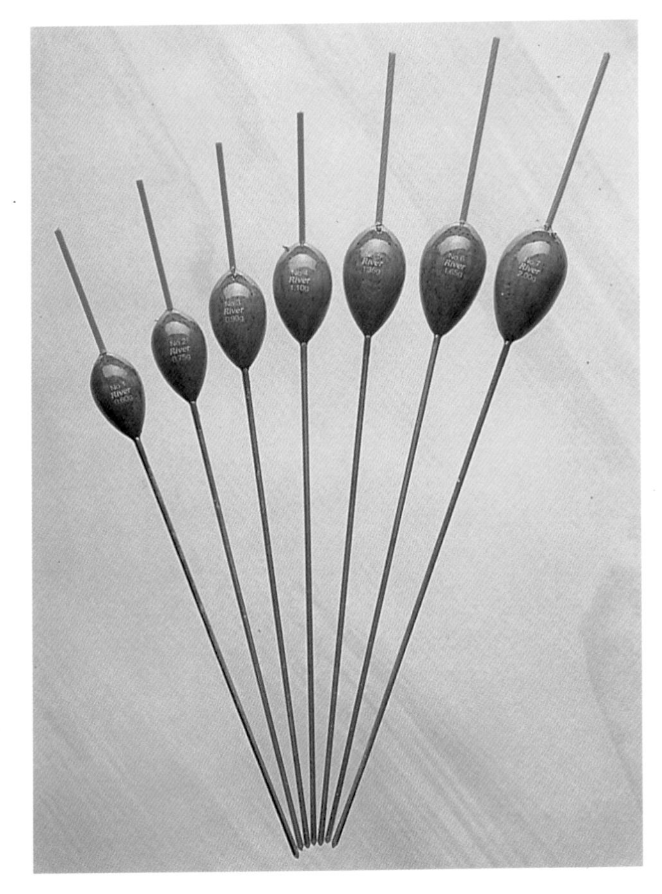

River floats should have bodies shaped like an upside-down pear.

bristle has been shotted so the body is fully submerged, it takes no more effort on the part of a fish to pull the bristle under. They're impossible to beat for sensitivity. So how come anglers don't use wire-bristled pole floats to the exclusion of all others? The main reason is that the bristle cannot be shotted in order that on-the-drop bites can be spotted. Once the body is submerged, the tiniest of tiny weights will sink the float out of sight. In fact, many anglers steer clear of them, claiming they are impossible to shot correctly. There is, however, a simple answer to the problem. By smearing a little grease – Mucilin is best – over the top part of the wire bristle, you will find that the float can be shotted much more easily. You are, in effect, shotting the grease. And what could be more sensitive than a float whose only above-water buoyancy is provided by a smear of grease on the wire bristle? Wire bristles can be difficult, but the rewards are there for the taking.

Recently introduced carbon bristles have exactly the same properties. Both types are often used right the way through the body of the float, the same material forming both bristle and stem. Like other types of bristle, their visibility can be improved by a coat of white base paint followed by one of a fluorescent top coat colour.

The length of bristle depends on the size of the float. Usually the heavier floats have the longest bristles, but this should cause no problems as long as you follow the simple rule: shot the float so that only the bristle – or even just part of it – is showing. If any of the float's body stands proud of the surface, it will lose sensitivity, and the main advantage of polefishing would be lost.

Of course, not all pole floats have bristles. 'Dibber'-type floats, such as those used for caster fishing on canals, are usually very short lengths of balsa or peacock quill with a small piece of wire glued into the bottom. The tops of the floats are simply the tops of the bodies, painted at the very tip to make them visible by the angler on the bank. These floats hold up well at the surface, when the bait is fished with several inches of line on the bottom, and they are not susceptible to being dragged under by any tow caused by flow or by the opening of lock gates – a common occurrence on canals. They work well in choppy conditions, too. Some anglers like pole floats without bristles for river fishing, claiming that bites are easier to detect and hit with just a tiny dimple of balsa body showing at the surface. These floats resemble conventional stick floats, with a slightly thinner body top.

Stems

Just as pole-float bristles come in several different materials, so do float stems – the long, thin length of material underneath the float body. By far the most popular material for stems is wire, which offers the desirable combination of strength, straightness and stability. The right sort of pole-float wire is much sought-after by manufacturers, and sources are often a closely guarded secret as it can make or break a pole float – literally. A long length of wire underneath a pole-float body provides much-needed stability in windy conditions, keeping the float upright despite the best efforts of the choppy upper layers of the water to tilt it this way and that. Line is attached by two or three short lengths of rubber sleeve – one directly underneath the body, one at the bottom and one half-way between. Choose a float with a wire stem for most polefishing applications, but they work particularly well in windy conditions, when using a long pole and short line, and for fishing on or very close to the bottom as they settle upright quickly once the 'bulk' has reached its level. Check that the wire on the floats you buy returns to the straight when you bend it slightly, and that it isn't rusty.

Another popular pole-float stem material is cane. A float with a cane stem works particularly well when you are fishing with a string of small shot or styl weights for fish feeding at all levels in the water, because its lightness helps the float 'tilt' as each shot settles. A wire-stemmed float would settle in a near-upright position, quickly making bite detection difficult. With a cane stem, however, it is fairly easy to detect when a fish intercepts the bait on the way down by its failure to settle properly. Cane-stemmed floats also 'cast' better than wire-stemmed ones, and are often used by anglers fishing to hand with a whip. A word of warning, however: cane-stemmed floats are very fragile – handle them with care, especially when altering depth by moving them up and down the line.

A fairly new addition to the range of pole-float stems is carbon. This material is sometimes preferable to either wire or cane in that it gives the angler the best of both worlds – it is stronger than cane, yet lighter than wire. It can be used for on-the-drop and to-hand fishing, yet there are no problems with the float breaking.

Body shapes

Pole-float bodies – that part of the float between bristle and stem – are usually made from balsa wood, but any light, buoyant material will do. One successful range of floats have bodies made from elder pith, while others are formed from man-made, dense polystyrene. Much more important than the materials from which pole-float bodies are made, is their shape, and more confusion surrounds this aspect of pole floats than any other.

Disregarding for a moment the size of the float, your choice of its body should be generally determined by two factors: flow and wind.

Many pole floats have bodies that can be broadly

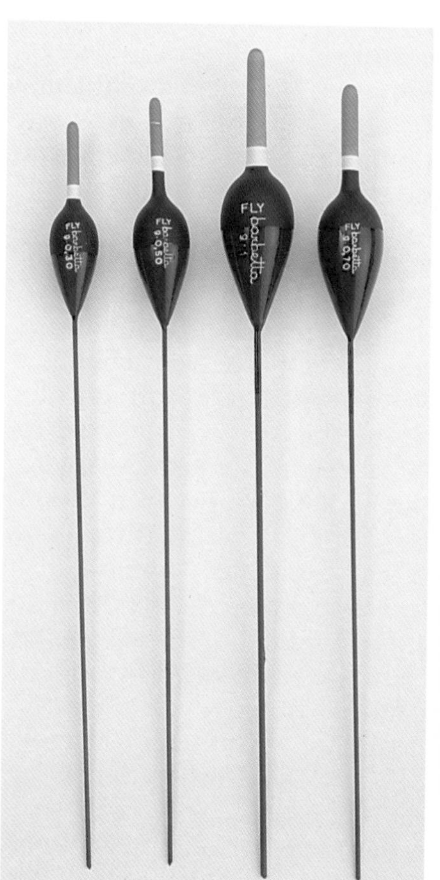

Some anglers prefer floats with no bristle especially on rivers.

Far right: the tips of these floats have been replaced with thicker bristles for better visibility.

described as looking like a pear, either the right way up or upside down. Let's look first at those whose body is like an upside-down pear. These are the floats for flowing water – the fatter the pear, the faster the water that the float will be able to handle. The reason is simple. A float with a body like an upside-down pear can be controlled much more easily in flowing water because it will not tend to rise out from the surface when its passage through the swim is slowed down or stopped by the angler. The pressure of water on the 'shoulder' of the float will, if anything, want to push it further underneath the surface. Slightly overshotted, these floats are perfect for river fishing, easing the bait through slower than the speed of the current for shy-biting roach.

On the other hand, floats whose bodies are shaped like a pear the right way up are better for still water or water that occasionally flows very slightly in either direction. These floats offer stability thanks to their low centre of gravity, and produce very little resistance on

Good quality fish like this carp caught by Jan Porter can be landed on the right pole tackle.

the strike because they are streamlined. They're highly sensitive, and in the smaller versions can be used on shallow canals, drains and ponds, and on lakes and very slowly-moving rivers in their larger versions.

In between these two extremes are many more patterns of pole float. There are floats with very long bodies, whose fattest part is at the bottom for windy conditions on stillwaters; floats whose bodies are almost spherical, which work well in windy conditions on rivers; floats with long, parallel bodies and long wire stems for stability and sensitivity; and highly sensitive floats with very long, slim bodies best-suited to no-wind, no-flow conditions; there are tiny, far-side canal floats for fishing overdepth in, sometimes, only 8 in of water. The list is almost endless, and it is all too easy to become confused, but the angler who remembers the 'pear' rule won't go far wrong when it comes to selecting pole floats.

Size

One of the great beauties about polefishing is the fact that very light, highly sensitive floats can be used. A swim that might need a rod-and-reel float taking three BBs just to cast the distance can be polefished with a float taking a fraction of that. Three BBs weigh in the region of 1.2 gm, but the same swim could be tackled with a pole float taking, say, 0.3 gm. Even so, many anglers still insist on using a float when polefishing that is far heavier than they need. It's all a question of creating a successful marriage for the considerations of depth, flow, species and wind. For example, a float taking just a few small shot might be best in a swim where the fish are feeding close to the surface, while bottom-feeding fish in the same swim should be tackled with something a little heavier, using most of the float's weight capacity as a 'bulk' close to the hook, with perhaps just one or two small shot as 'droppers' underneath. Similarly, although a light float might work in one swim in calm conditions, a much heavier one might be required when it's windy to achieve good tackle control without the wind blowing float – and bait – around. If in doubt, start with a float a little on the light side – many anglers new to polefishing make the mistake of using floats which are too heavy.

CHAPTER FOUR

MAKING WINDERS

There are two schools of thought when it comes to tackle for polefishing. Some anglers spend hours on end at home, lovingly preparing their pole tackle, shotting floats, selecting and measuring line and wrapping the finished product around specially-made plastic pole-winders, which they then store in neat rows in their boxes. They're the envy of their friends and can be ready to fish in a matter of minutes. Others would rather do everything on the bankside, taking their time to select the float, line and hook they want from those in their box and getting everything exactly right for the session on which they are about to embark. Both approaches have their staunch supporters and opposers. Some wouldn't even consider going fishing without a pristine collection of more than 50 winders prepared to perfection, while others don't have a single one in their box.

If the beginner to polefishing wants to do everything right, he should fall somewhere between the two. The angler with 60 winders will probably admit to using only 20 of them during the course of a season, while the angler who hasn't a single pole rig ready will at times probably regret not being able to get fishing quickly. Anyway, making up pole rigs at home is great fun and provides a sound grounding into the skills of polefishing.

There are many things to be considered when you want to make up rigs at home. These range from the float you want to use, to the line, type of shotting, and the length of the rig itself. In addition to this, you must have an easy way of discovering just what your chosen float takes in the way of shotting, without the advantage of a stretch of water in front of you into which to drop the float and shot. Fortunately, the answer to this

Completed pole winders make an attractive addition to an anglers tackle.

Far right: the well-prepared pole angler can be catching fish within minutes of arriving at the waterside.

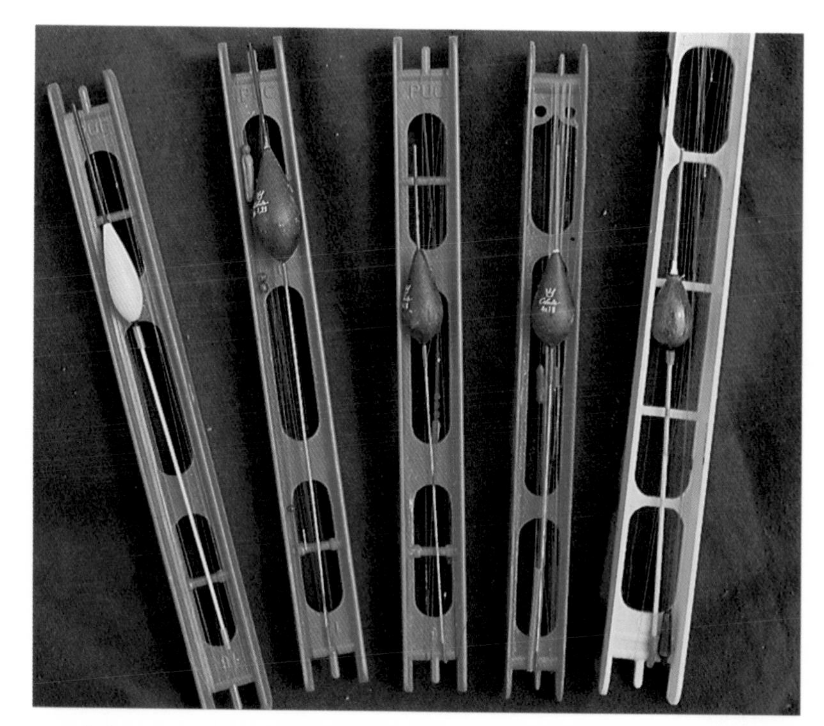

problem is easy, thanks to special neutral-buoyancy devices. The best-known are the Dosa Piombo and the Nutroboy, and they really are easy to use. Instead of fixing weights on to the line, you simply slot your float into the top of the devise, place shot, styls or olivette in the saucer around its edge, and lower the lot into a bucket of water. By adding or subtracting weights, you can shot the float perfectly. All you then have to do is fix the same float and weights on to your line and you know that the float will be shotted very accurately. You can make minor adjustments on the riverbank.

With the first problem out of the way, let's look at the other decisions you must take when making rigs at home.

Line

Line for polefishing does not have to withstand the same pressure as line for fishing with a rod and reel. No casting power is needed, and no brute strength required to beat fish – the pressure is largely taken up by the elastic when a long pole is used. For this reason, line for polefishing should generally be lighter than that for use with rods and reels. Where a reel line of 2 lb to 2½ lb breaking strain might be used for casting a waggler or a

DELCAC

stick float into the river, the same swim could be tackled easily with a pole line of 1½ lb breaking strain. As long as the right knots are used, the pole angler should never be broken when using a main pole line of this strength, except in very unusual circumstances, such as when a very large fish is hooked. Even then, the elastic will do its work and the fish can still be landed by a combination of skill, experience and a little luck.

The situation has been improved – and somewhat complicated – in recent years by the influx of so-called high-tech lines into Britain. These lines are nothing like traditional monofilament. They boast extremely fine diameters for a given breaking strain, offering the angler obvious advantages: he can use the same diameter line as before, which gives him more strength in his line; or he can use the same breaking strain as before, which gives him a much thinner line. Thin lines are less likely to be seen by the fish than thick lines, so why are low-diameter lines not used exclusively for every type of fishing?

The answer lies in their other properties. Most high-tech, low-diameter lines are pre-stretched. This certainly makes then thinner while retaining a good degree of strength, but it it also removes most of the line's stretch. For rod-and-reel fishing, a line must be able to stretch considerably or it will be broken easily when the angler casts or strikes – that is why pre-stretched lines should not be used on the reel. Such requirements of are not so important for the pole angler, however. Line stretch is not so vital as long as some sort of shock-absorber is used in the form of elastic or flick-tip. So the pole angler has another weapon in his armoury – the potential to use line of a much thinner diameter than his rod-and-reel counterpart. As an example, a typical, conventional line of 1½ lb breaking strain will have a diameter of 0.1 mm. A typical high-tech, low-diameter line of the same

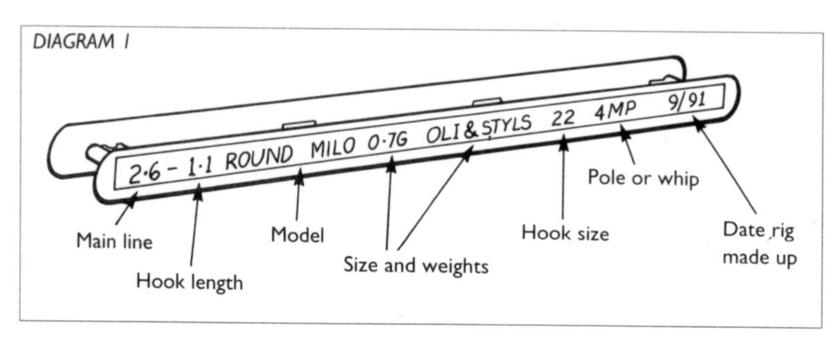

Some anglers like to label their winders so they know exactly what they are using.

breaking strain, however, will measure just 0.08 mm. That might not seem much variance, but to a match angler fishing for hundreds of pounds, it could make the difference between winning and finishing among the also-rans.

Learn to view lines not just by breaking strain, but by diameter as well as they have been doing on the Continent for many years. It makes the whole question of lines much simpler. Don't feel obliged to use high-tech lines, however. Many people have tried high-tech lines as main line for polefishing and reverted back to conventional lines. Special knots often have to be used, the line has be extremely well looked after as it is highly abrasive, and many think it just isn't worth the trouble.

Hooklengths are different, however, and high-tech lines are perfect in this department. With diameters as little as 0.05 mm, they are hardly visible with the human eye, let along that of the fish! The beginner is best advised to use ordinary, good-quality line for his main pole line, but high-tech, low-diameter lines are worth trying for hooklengths. Don't worry if you can't get on at all with them, however – 12 oz hooklengths of non-stretched lines are normally perfectly adequate unless matchfishing. As a guide, use 1½ lb breaking strain line for main line and 12 oz for hooklengths.

On the subject of lines, another decision you will have to make when it comes to rigs is the actual length of line to wrap around the winder. The first point to remember, obviously, is the depth of water for which the float and shotting is designed. If you intend fishing a 6-ft deep river swim with your rig, it's pointless making the rig with just 6 ft of line – there will be no extra line between the tip of the pole and the float. If you work on the basis of at least 1 yd between poletip and float, you'll see that at least 9 ft of line will be required in this situation, although as we're talking about a river here you could even go further than that, and have even more line on your rig to allow the float to travel more of the swim without reaching its limit. Similarly, if you intend fishing a shallow canal or pond of only 3 ft deep, making a rig with 6 ft of line will be about right.

Some anglers don't like to be restricted to certain lengths, and use the same length of line – say, 15 ft – with all their rigs. They then shorten the line accordingly having decided how much they want when they reach

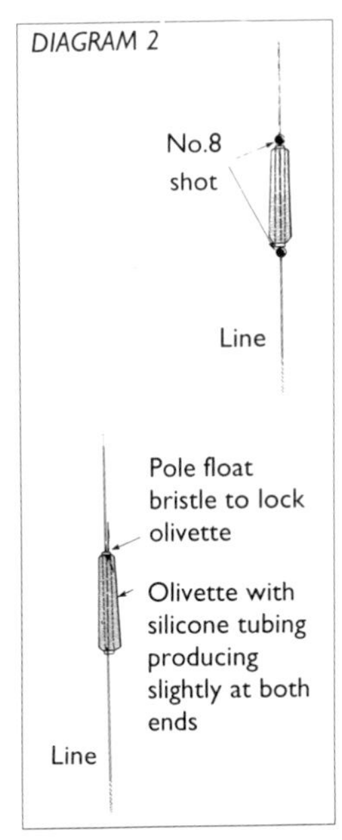

Olivettes are secured either by shot (top) or short piece of bristle.

their swim. This is a good idea, but problems can occur when they need to add line to a rig – extra line can be tied on at the top of the rig but knots are an unwelcome encumbrance on fine pole tackle. The fewer knots the better.

Although we're talking about line length in feet, in actual fact the right way to measure line for your pole rigs is against your pole – and the only way to do this, is to lay your pole out and measure the line against the number of sections you want it to equal in length. Pole lines must correspond to the end of one section and the start of another, so that a fish can be lifted safely to hand or easily netted without having to reach up or down – a recipe for disaster. The wrong length of line is an all too common mistake made even by good pole anglers.

Rigs

Making up pole rigs at home is an enjoyable occupation and can while away many otherwise boring closed-season evenings.

■ **STEP 1**
The things you'll need are: a bucket of water, a float, a winder that has been tested against the float to make sure the float sits neatly inside with no protruding ends, line, weights (olivette, styls and shot), styl pincers, tweezers, pole-float shotter (this is the Preston Innovations Nutroboy), scissors and pole anchor (for attaching completed rig to winder).
Take the bottom of the pole float and push it into the hole in the centre of the Nutroboy. All sizes of pole-float stem can be used with the Nutroboy, but make sure it is well-secured.

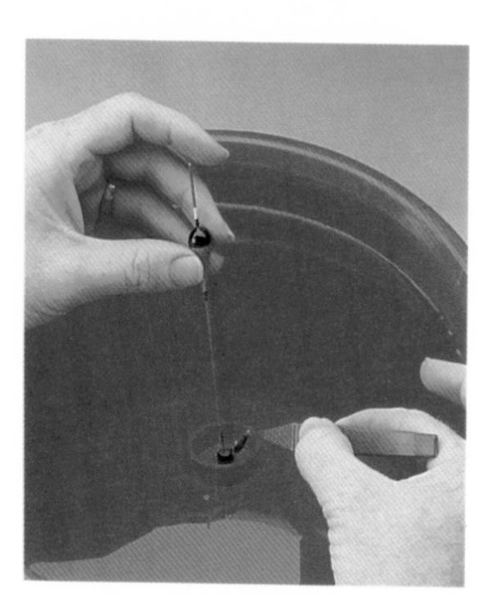

■ **STEP 2**
Start dropping weights into the Nutroboy, beginning with the largest. This float takes 1 gm and you want to shot it with an olivette and styl weights. So a 0.8-gm olivette goes in just (special tweezers are supplied with the Nutroboy), followed by a No.8 shot to prevent it sliding to the hook. It's a good idea to add in a No.10 shot as well. This goes above the olivette to secure it and stop it sliding up to the float when baiting the hook.
Test the float in the bucket of water, adding or taking away styl weights until you achieve the setting you want. Undershot the float slightly to allow for the weight of the baited hook and line – polefishing is a delicate business. Final minor adjustments can be made on the bankside.

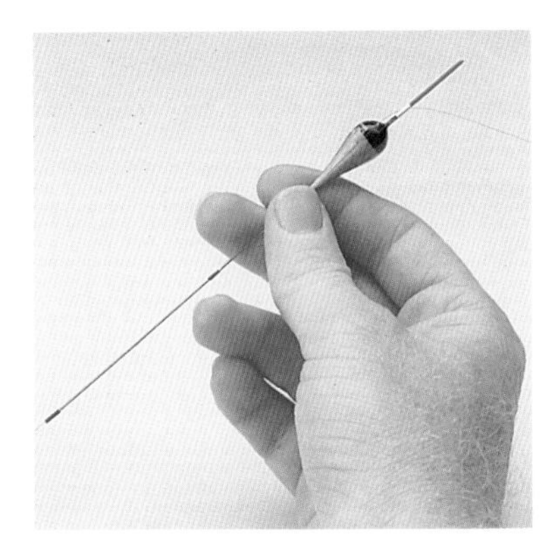

■ STEP 3
When you are happy with the setting of the float, remove it from the Nutroboy and keep the weights safe. Measure the line against the length of pole to which you want it to correspond, and thread the float up the line from the bottom. Use two soft but tight pieces of silicone rubber on the stem, one immediately under the body and one at the end of the stem. Really long-stemmed floats should be secured with three rubbers. With the float on the line, slide the olivette up from the bottom and secure it with the No.8 shot underneath and the No.10 above. The fattest part of the olivette is furthest away from the float. Don't squeeze them too tightly as you will probably want to move the olivette before you start fishing. Start with it around 3 ft from the hook.

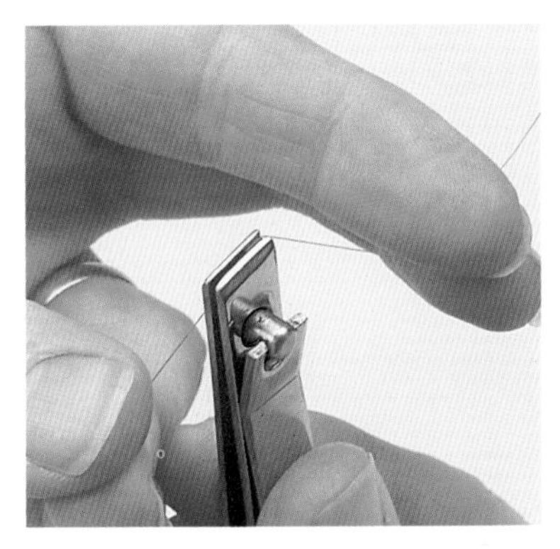

■ STEP 4
As many styl weights are added to the Nutroboy to make the float sit correctly. These are fixed on to the line with styl pincers. The three styls here are equally spaced between olivette and the bottom end of the line. Again, they can be moved on the riverbank. Once all the weights have been fixed on to the line, tie a loop in both ends and slip the bottom loop (the one underneath the float) over the peg at one end of the winder. Carefully wind the rig around the winder, moving the float up or down slightly so it sits neatly in the winder protected from possible damage.

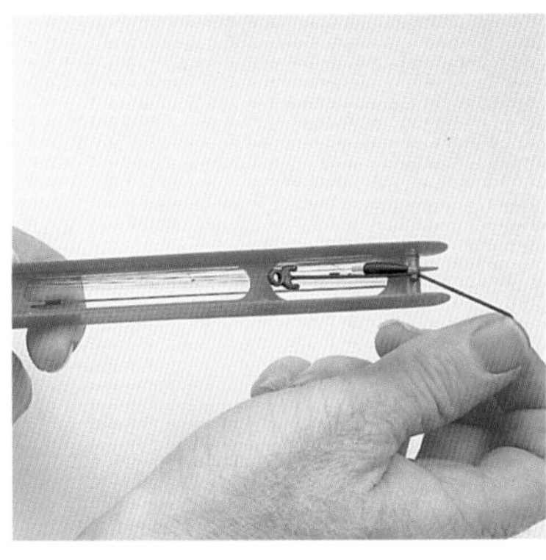

■ STEP 5
Continue until all the line is wound on to the winder. Place the anchor end of an elasticated pole anchor through the loop and secure. Stretch and wrap the anchor around the winder, securing the other end of it around the first available peg in one end. It's worth making a note of the length of rig on the side of the winder so that it is immediately recognisable. Some anglers add other details such as line strength, float shotting capacity, type of shotting and the date.

You'll notice no hook or hooklength has been tied to the winder. Some anglers prefer their pole rigs on winders to be stored complete with hooks, but it's better to leave hooks off them. Hooks rust with just a couple of drops of water, and fine polefishing hooklengths are easily damaged when they are stored in a box. It's better to keep your hooks and hooklengths separately, tying them at home and looking after them in small individual packets.

Winders

One pole winder might look very much like another, but it's worth checking on a few small but important points before making your selection. Winders come in numerous different lengths and it is imperative that you make sure they are longer than the floats they are to take. Your floats will quickly become damaged if they protrude from either end of the winder. Take care also with floats that have big, bulky bodies. With floats like these it is best to use wider winders whose centre panels are nearer to one side than the other. Make sure the float sits in the deepest side to avoid damage. Make sure as well that the winder is wide enough to allow the float to sit inside the two edges, otherwise they will cut its body. Finally, you might want to choose the colour of your winders according to the length of line wrapped around them, or the type of rig. This will make identification easier when you are faced with lots of winders in your tackle tray.

Ready-made pole rigs should be stored carefully. Not only is it important to keep them away from heat and light, which rots fine lines quickly, but you should also make sure that the winders cannot rattle about in your box – another way to damage the delicate rigs on them. It's no coincidence that Continental-type tackle boxes have become more popular in Britain since polefishing really took off. These boxes have one or more shallow trays incorporated into their lid section which are ideal for the safe storage of pole winders. They look good in them as well!

Olivettes, shot and styls

Until you decide to start polefishing, you will probably never have encountered olivettes. An olivette, simply, is a streamlined weight that is often used on pole rigs instead of several weights, which might be more prone to tangling. It ensures that the bait gets down quickly to where you want it, and is probably the best bet when the intention is to fish on or very close to the bottom all day.

Most olivettes are tubular in construction with the fattest part at the bottom, and line is threaded through the middle and secured either end by small split shot, styls or with a small length of pole-float bristle. They are available in sizes from 0.1 gm to more than 10 gm in weight, and between olivette and hook, one or more small shot or styl weights, called droppers, are fixed. Both olivette and droppers can be moved up and down during the course of the session. The most popular olivettes are made from tungsten and many now come supplied with soft silicone tubing threaded through their centres. This tubing acts as a buffer at either end against abrasion. Other types include olivettes that secure the line at either end with very small pieces of silicone rubber. These olivettes are easily moved up and down the line. Only one olivette is used on a rig.

Shot

Olivettes are fine when you will be catching fish on or very close to the bottom all day, but what about those days when the fish might feed at all levels in the water? In these conditions, olivettes can easily make you miss out on fish taking the bait 'on the drop', or as it falls through the water. The olivette simply pulls the bait down too fast. This is one of the reasons why more and more anglers are turning to shot to weight their pole floats. Shot can be used as bulk, fixed closely together to perform a similar – if slightly inferior – function to an olivette, or they can be spread out to produce a slower fall of the bait through the water. Shot are certainly the simplest way of setting a float and anglers like them for their versatility. For most polefishing situations, it's best to use shot no larger than No 8. The higher the number, the smaller the shot.

Weight guide:

No.8	0.063 gm
No.9	0.049 gm
No.10	0.034 gm
No.12	0.02 gm
No.13	0.012 gm

Styls

Styls are small, cylindrical weights with a split running along their length. They become flat when fixed on to line and are much used by pole anglers when they are after the most delicate presentation possible. With care they can be moved up and down the line to make bulk and strung-out rigs, and the best styls for polefishing are those between No.12 and No.7. Unlike shot, the larger the number, the larger the styl. They are often also used when trying to catch with hempseed on the hook. Fish can easily mistake a round split shot for a grain of hempseed, taking the shot in their mouth and causing false bites – called shot bites. With styls there are no such problems. A fish mistaking a styl weight for a grain of hemp has to be very stupid indeed!

Weight guide:

No.12	0.064 gm
No.11	0.048 gm
No.10	0.035 gm
No.9	0.025 gm
No.8	0.017 gm
No. 7	0.01 gm

As you can see, styl weights are very tiny indeed – a No.8 split shot weighs 0.063 gm, almost exactly the same as a No.12 styl – and there are five styl weights smaller than that! It follows that for really delicate

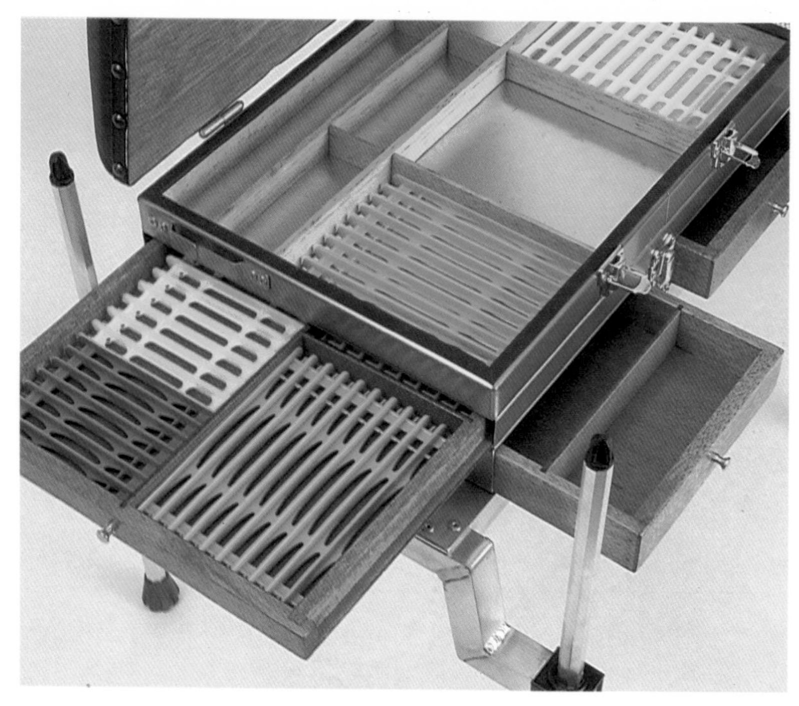

Continental-type tackle boxes are designed like this one to hold many pole winders.

presentation of a floatfished bait, as is often required in polefishing, styl weights can prove extremely useful. With the bristle on most pole floats being extremely fine and sensitive, often a No.7 styl is all that's required to sink them from the top of the body to the top of the nylon bristle. Styls are often used as 'dropper' weights underneath the bulk of an olivette or several styls grouped closely together.

A little practise is required to fix styl weights on the line, but once you've mastered it, the process takes just a few seconds. Special, tailor-made styl pincers are a must.

1 Slide several styls from the dispenser and gently grasp one that is lying with the split downwards with the pincers.

2 Pick up the styl with the pincers, ensuring that you don't accidentally squeeze the two sides together.

3 Make sure your line is tight by pulling it under pressure, and carefully slip it into the split of the styl.

4 Now just squeeze the pincers and the styl will be lying neatly on the line. Don't squeeze it too hard or you won't be able to move it up and down the line.

A styl weight can even be removed with care, by pulling it away from the line so that the line is forced out of the split. As long as it's been fixed on properly, the line will remain undamaged.

Above: special boxes are available for completed winders.

Left: some anglers like to have dozens of pole winders lovingly prepared at home.

CHAPTER FIVE

THE RIGS TO USE

Ask a dozen experienced pole anglers which type of rig they prefer and the chances are you will get 12 different answers. There are few hard-and-fast rules in polefishing, and a rig and shotting pattern that works well for one angler might not be as effective for another. But as you become more experienced in this branch of angling, you will soon learn that certain rigs are best used for certain conditions and certain species, and it is the angler who succeeds in working out what's best in several departments who catches the most. Only after examining several different conditions should you make your final choice from the rigs you have available, or what tackle to set up on the bank.

It is useful to look at several imaginary fishing situations and decide what's best for each one. Read each one and then adapt the suggestions to your own requirements.

Rivers

Flow – moderate
Depth – 6 ft at 9 m out
Wind – slight

There are several different ways in which the pole angler can tackle a swim such as this one on a river. First, you must decide on your choice of floats. As discussed in Chapter Three, the best floats for flowing water have a slight shoulder at the top of the body which allows the angler to control them easily. By this is meant slowing down the passage of the float through the swim by slowing down the movement of the pole as it follows the float. As the line tightens between pole-tip and float, so will the float slow down or stop. Slim pole floats, or pole floats whose bodies have their fattest parts at the bottom, would soon 'ride' out a little way above the water surface, ruining their effectiveness. However, floats whose bodies have a slight shoulder will be forced downwards by the current and stay where you want them. Use a fatter-bodied float in faster water, and a slimmer one in slower flows, and for the best results add a little more shot than you would under normal circumstances if you want to hold them back hard – usually this is not necessary except in flood conditions, however.

Having selected the pattern of float you want to use, it's time to choose its weight-carrying capacity. The swim is 6 ft deep so that immediately gives you some idea – and here's where many beginners to polefishing make their first big mistake. Just because they would use a waggler taking three AAAs in 6 ft of water, they select a pole float taking the equivalent of three AAAs – and that's much too heavy. Three AAAs weigh roughly 2½ gm, but your pole-float choice should take less than half that. Now you can begin to see why polefishing has numerous advantages – if you can catch using a three AAA float, imagine what you will catch using one taking a third as much!

Below: three ways for rivers. Pole-float shotting patterns.

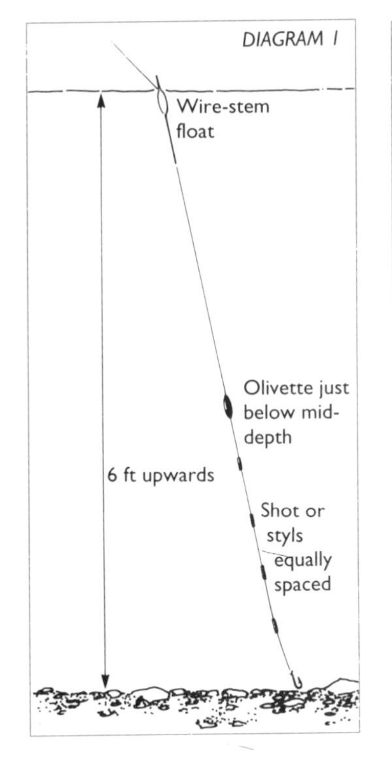

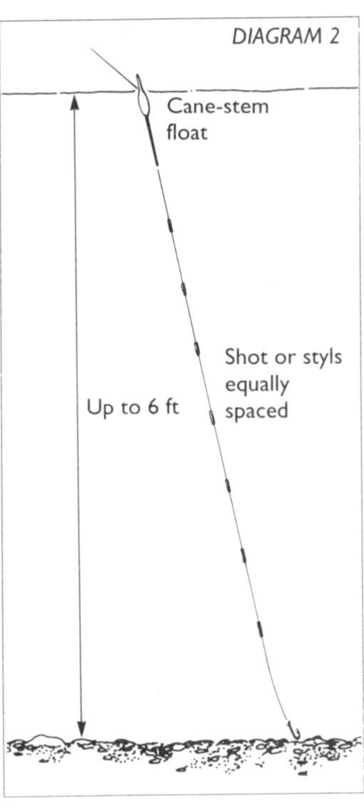

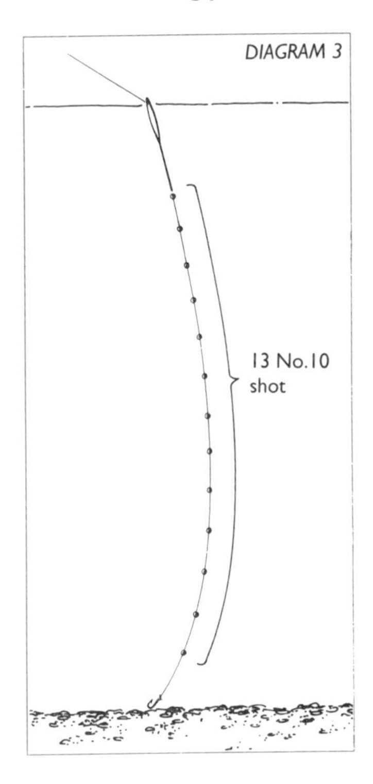

Small rivers can be perfectly fished with a pole. South London angler Andy Love prepares to net a fish from Surrey's River Mole.

For our imaginary swim you should be looking at a float taking in the region of 0.6 gm to 1 gm. Your actual final choice should be determined by the strength and direction of the wind as well as your chosen style of shotting. Let's look at wind first. If the wind is nothing more than a gentle breeze blowing in a downstream direction or from behind you, you will have few problems and can almost disregard it when it comes to float size choice. However, too light a float can pose problems in a wind blowing in an upstream direction, or into your face. In these conditions, you will probably need to use a larger float to give you the stability to move in the right direction. If the flow is slight, too light a float in either of these two wind conditions will simply not 'pick up' the flow and the chances of a good catch are reduced. In stronger flows, an upstream wind will not pose so much of a problem. The answer is to use a float that takes enough weight to combat the wind, but one where there is no excess shotting, which is wasted.

What about the style of shotting? There are several options here, ranging from the use of an olivette to styl weights – and a combination of the two – but the basic choice the angler has to make is whether to use a bulk rig or a strung-out one. Rigs that are described as bulk rigs are those which have most of the float's shotting capacity bulked together at or below mid-depth, while strung-out rigs have several smaller weights fixed at equal distances from each other, either all the way from float to hook, or in the bottom part of the rig.

Many pole anglers would opt for a bulk rig in our imaginary swim, choosing an olivette to be fixed around 2½ ft from the hook, followed by several small styl weights between the olivette and the hook. In this instance, four styl weights of sizes 10, 9, 8 and 7, with the No.7 nearest the hook, would be about right.

This is the simplest way of tackling this swim and it would undoubtedly catch you fish. Choosing a float taking about 0.8 gm would be right. The olivette would pull your hookbait quickly through the water until it reached its settling point, after which the styls would produce a slower, more natural fall through the bottom section of water. The rig would allow fish to intercept the bait from around mid-depth right to the bottom, and the olivette can be moved closer to the hook if the fish are feeding close to the riverbed. However, the big

A string of shot is often better than an olivette.

Fish like chub can be landed on a pole. This one was hooked by top matchman Dave Harrell.

disadvantage of an olivette is that it cannot be separated out, and this is why lots of good pole anglers now rarely use them, except for deep water or fishing for bream or eels. Instead of the olivette, they would much prefer the versatility offered by split shot, which can be bulked together or strung out as required. They're not as neat as an olivette, but they certainly offer the angler more versatility. It's all about experimentation – an olivette rig might work on one day, but on the next day the same swim might respond best to a strung-out rig.

The third point for the angler to consider is line length. With a moderate flow, a depth of 6 ft and little wind, you would do well to use a rig length corresponding to the top five sections of your pole. Most top five sections will equal around 15 ft long, so taking away the 6 ft between float and hook, you are left with 9 ft of line between float and pole tip. This is much too much for stillwaters, but on a flowing river that extra 9 ft will mean that you can use most of your swim, following the float at it goes. In windy conditions, that 9 ft might have to be shortened, as it would if the river was moving very slowly and most fish were being caught at the upstream end of it. In that case, the extra line would simply get in the way. Don't just sit there, if the line length needs altering, do it! It only takes a minute or so to remove the line from the top of the pole, cut through it and remove or add about 3 ft. Remember that we are talking about a swim that's 6 ft deep – you'll need more line still if it's deeper, or less if it's shallower.

Lakes

Depth – 8 ft at 11 m out
Wind – strong

Let us assume that this imaginary lake is full of bream, roach and tench that live close to the bank. They are great fun to catch on pole tackle, but only if you present your tackle to them in the right way. Choice of float is just as important as it is on a river, but on a lake there's little flow to worry about. Lakes do flow in one sense, of course, when the lower part of the water moves in the opposite direction to the wind, which is pushing the top part towards one bank. When this top part of the water has nowhere else to go, having hit the bank, it

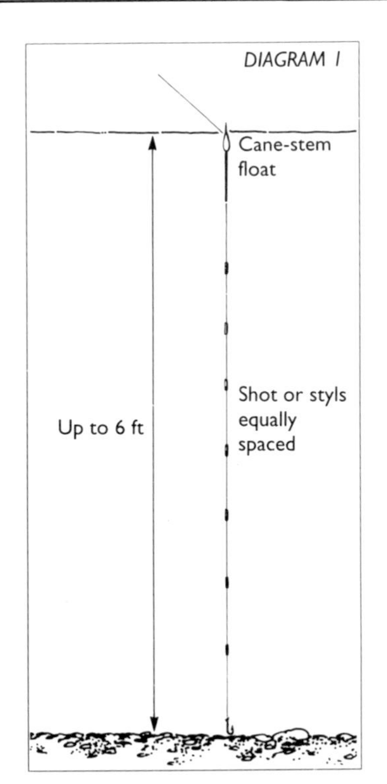

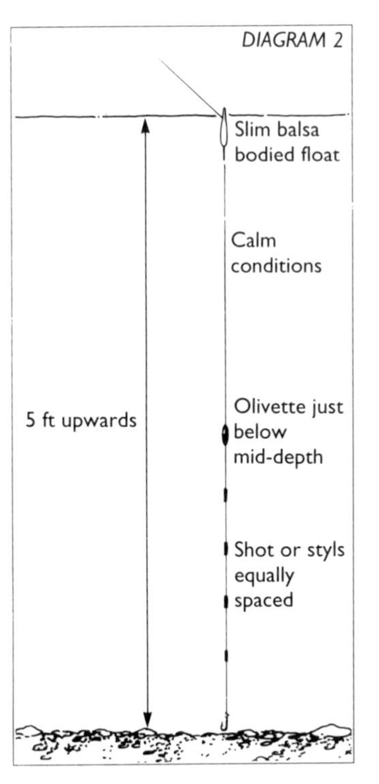

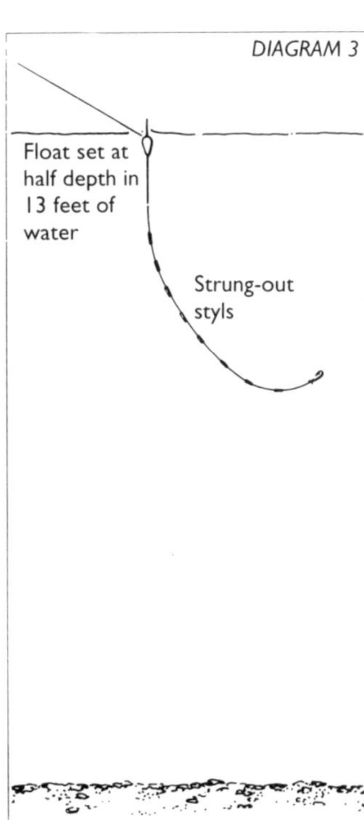

Above: three typical lake pole-float shotting patterns.

turns under and moves in the opposite direction. It is something to be aware of, but rarely will the undertow be so strong that you need to use a float with a shoulder like those you should use on rivers.

In fact, a typical stillwater float has a body that is an upside-down copy of the river float – instead of being fattest at the top, it's fattest at the bottom. This fattest part of the body provides the float with stability, and the lower down the float it is, the greater the stability that is offered. It's absolutely no use trying to polefish a windy lake with a float that is being blown around all over the place. A long wire or carbon stem also helps the float's stability, serving the same purpose as those floats with long, tapered bodies that were popular a few years ago. For our windy lake, in 8 ft of water, a float taking between 1 and 1½ gm would be about right. As conditions worsen, use a bigger float.

Fishing for mainly bottom feeders like bream and tench demands a bait fished on or very close to the bottom, and a strung-out rig is therefore no use. The angler's first choice might be an olivette fixed towards the bottom end of the line, with one or more droppers underneath in the form of small shot or styl weights. It's unlikely you will need the delicacy of half a dozen

Worsbrough Reservoir near Barnsley, S.Yorks. A superb lake for the poles.

strategically placed styl weights – just one or two should suffice. If you are fishing with 6 in of line on the bottom – an excellent way of catching good-quality fish in lakes – it might pay to rest a No.8 or No.10 shot just on the bottom. Bites will often be slight lifts of the float here.

Other species – and even tench – will sometimes come up in lakes to feed close to the surface, and for this a different type of rig is required. First, you'll need a much lighter float. Second, there's no need for an olivette. Just use a float taking 0.5 gm at most and shot it with round split shot or styl weights, strung out between float and hook. A cane-stemmed float is ideal for this sort of fishing, because it will tilt slowly in the water as each small weight settles and registers. Bites will be seen either as the float failing to settle, or shooting away out of sight – and then the fun starts! When casting this type of rig, make sure the tackle is laid out on the water in a straight line. Roach, skimmer bream and carp are typical species that will come up to feed close to the surface, especially on a hot summer day. Keep them happy with generous helpings of maggot loosefeed, dropping your hookbait among them.

Length of line on stillwaters should be determined mainly by two factors – wind and water clarity. In ideal conditions, the best advice is to use roughly 3 ft of line between float and pole-tip. This will give you enough line to allow for a little pole-tip movement, when feeding, for example, without upsetting the float. The exceptions to the 3-ft rule are when it's windy – more line will probably be required to prevent the wind blowing the pole-tip around, pulling the float around as well; and when the water is clear. Shy fish are easily spooked by a length of unnatural material waving

Many lakes are tailor-made for poles. This is Moorlands Farm near Kidderminster.

around over their heads. It is amazing what can be seen from the bottom of an 8 ft deep swim.

Canals and drains

There are several different ways of fishing canals and drains with a pole, all of which require slightly different rigs made up either in advance or on the bank. It would be useful here to talk about species and baits rather than conditions, as the basic rigs will stay roughly the same regardless of wind strength, although the float shape and size should be altered following the same general guidelines as those already suggested for rivers and lakes.

The first point to remember is that you should always use the smallest float that will give you adequate control – in fact, this is a good policy to adopt for 90 per cent of polefishing, whatever the venue. However, there is an exception – small, bottom-feeding fish like gudgeon on canals can sometimes be caught at great speed by anglers using floats taking a surprisingly large amount of weight. It's nothing to see them with floats of 1 gm, or even more, fishing whips 3 m from the bank. These floats are of the stillwater type, with bodies whose fattest parts are at the bottom, and they're shotted with an olivette only a few inches from the hook and one, or at most two, droppers in the form of No.8 or No.10 shot below. The tackle is dropped into the water right under the end of the whip, and seconds later another gudgeon or ruffe is in the net. Many 'towpath' anglers who specialise in this sort of fishing like to use floats with

The best way of tackling the far shelf of a canal.

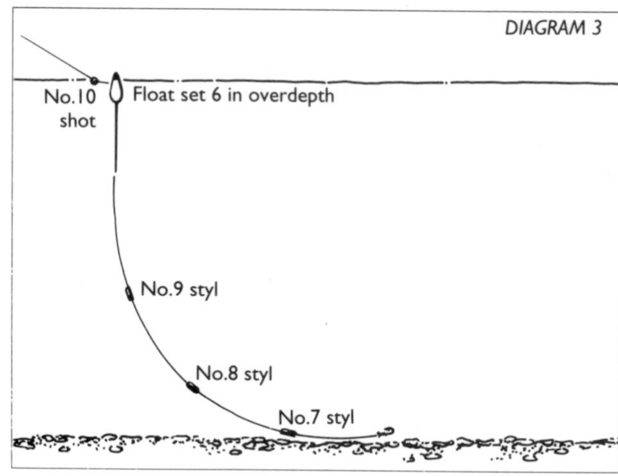

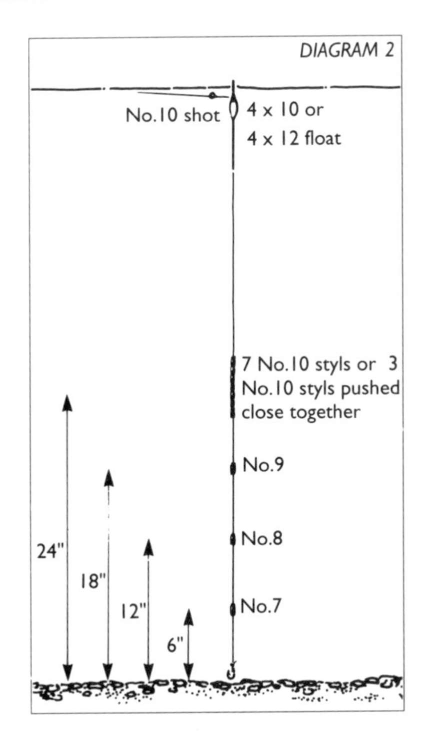

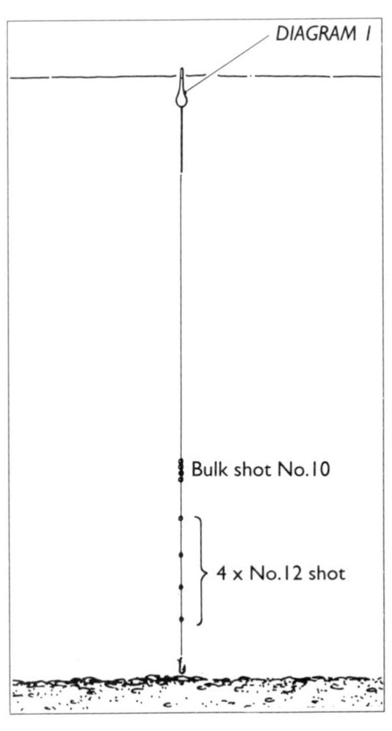

Two shotting patterns for canals and drains.

cane bristles as opposed to nylon or wire ones. These cane bristles are slightly more buoyant, and if a fish intercepts the bait after the olivette has settled but before the droppers have, the bite will be easy to see by the failure of the cane tip to settle.

What about fishing for roach on canals and other small waters? With small baits like squatts and pinkies, the best type of rig to use is one composed of shot or styl weights – and here styl weights definitely have the edge in terms of delicacy of presentation and effectiveness. A favoured float type has a simple, rugby-ball-shaped body and wire stem and takes in the region of four No.12 or four No.14 styls – that's roughly 0.25 gm and 0.4 gm respectively. Don't fall into the trap of believing that just because a float suggests it takes four No.12 styls, that's exactly what you should fix on the line. It's far better to split these styls further to allow more, but smaller weights to shot the float. In a 3 to 4 ft deep swim, try fixing a No.7, No.8 and No.9 styl weight at 3, 6 and 9 in from the hook, followed at just below mid-depth by a string of No.10 styls fixed so they are just touching each other to weight the float right to the tip. This rig gives you the best of both worlds – it allows a slow drop of the bait in the bottom half of the water to catch roach from mid-depth onwards, and the small bulk of styl weights can be separated if required to provide a slow fall throughout the whole depth.

That's a popular rig for catching roach, but what about the swim you've chosen that has a lovely looking bush opposite, which you think might be home to some big roach, and even a chub or carp as well? Here, there's no bait to beat casters, and canal anglers have developed a highly successful rig for fishing with them. These big fish will usually want a bait presented right on the bottom, but the problem with conventional, bristle-tipped pole floats is that if there's any wind or tow caused by the opening and closing of locks, the bristle will be constantly pulled under and bites will be impossible to spot.

The answer is to use a different type of float, with no bristle but a thicker, more buoyant tip made from material such as peacock quill or balsa. Not only are these floats buoyant and ideal for combating wind and tow when fished overdepth, they are also easy to see

At 11 m wide this is a typical canal venue and ideal for the pole.

Left: right in the town centre canals offer the pole angler the chance of good sport.

when shotted correctly so that only the barest tip is visible at the surface. These floats are usually tiny, short, stubby affairs, ideal for the sometimes very shallow water they will be used in. And they take only a few shot or styls. Plumb the depth carefully, and then move the float so that at least 6 in of line is on the bottom. At least one tiny weight should be allowed to lie on the bottom as well, but be prepared to go deeper, with more weight on the bottom if the wind or tow increases. The trick is to reach the ideal combination of perfect tackle control and successful bite-to-fish ratio – big canal roach have a habit of giving seemingly perfect bites but avoiding being caught – usually because the angler is fishing with too much line on the bottom. A typical shotting pattern for this type of fishing would be a No.9, No.8 and No.7 styl (or the equivalent in round split shot) weight equally spaced between float and hook (smallest nearest the hook and on the bottom). Scant caster loosefeed and caster on the hook should then do the damage.

Lancastrian Dave Roper used casters to take this fine bream catch on the pole from the Lancaster Canal.

What line length should you use for these types of waters? Two to three feet is ideal, but use more in windy conditions so that the movement of the pole-tip won't drag the float off line, and when the water is clear. Shallow-canal fish are very easily scared.

Backshotting

In windy conditions, there is still a way to use a long

pole successfully, even if the effect of the wind on the pole is making your tackle blow around all over the place. It's called backshotting and you might have heard of stick-float anglers using it.

Backshotting means fixing a weight above your float to sink part of the line out of the way of the wind. It serves two purposes. First, by sinking the line, the waves caused by the wind on the surface do not catch hold of it and pull the float all over the place. Second, if the wind blows the pole-tip around, most of the movement is taken up by the backshot, not the float; the float and bait remain relatively stable. The size and position of a backshot is determined to a large extent by the wind. Start by using a No.10, just a couple of inches above the float. If this doesn't help keep it still, increase the size of the weight and move it further up the line towards the pole-tip. The extreme in backshotting is reached when you fix an AAA shot just a couple of feet under the tip of the pole (remember that as it is windy, you will using at least 6 ft of line between pole tip and float). By holding the pole so that this shot is kept just off the water's surface, it won't pull the float under, but will help it remain relatively stable by absorbing most of the movement caused by the wind blowing the tip around. Get the balance right and you can achieve a high degree of control. With smaller backshot placed closer to the hook, you will need to take the equivalent weight from under the float or it will be pulled under. Some anglers allow for this by incorporating a small backshot in all of their rigs, fixing it right next to the top ring of the float and only using it as a backshot when they need to.

Hooklengths

A word about hooklengths. Because much of polefishing requires weights to be placed close to the hook, it is advisable to use short hooklengths. As ultra-fine lines are much used for pole hooklengths, it is not a good idea to fix any shot on them. For that reason, many pole anglers use hooklengths of only 6 in or so, attaching them to the main line by the two-loop knot. Sometimes they go even shorter, if they want to place a shot or styl really close to the hook. Try this when polefishing for bottom-feeders like gudgeon.

CHAPTER SIX

STARTING OFF

You've now done the hardest part. You've bought your pole and floats and have made your decisions over the rigs you intend to to use. Perhaps you have them neatly lined up on pole-winders in your box, or maybe you've just a dozen or so floats, which you can make into rigs on the riverbank. Now it's down to the important part – fishing! Even so, the job will be much easier if you have a few specially made polefishing accessories.

First, beginners to polefishing usually like to use a pole rest, and there's nothing at all wrong with that. A pole rest consists of two supports, which attach to one side of your box – if you are right-handed, they attach on the right side. One of the U-shaped supports hooks around the top of the pole very close to the butt, while the other supports it from underneath, 1 ft or so further along. The best ones are adjustable so that the pole can be slipped in, leaving it in exactly the right position – with the tip just above the water. They really are a boon for the beginner to polefishing when it comes to feeding, as you can place the pole in the rest, leaving both hands free. However, as you will see later, there are other methods of feeding while still holding your pole. Make sure the rest has wide supports with no sharp metal edges and you won't go far wrong. Don't place your fully extended pole in its rest and then stand up – all that will happen is that your pole-tip will smack on to the water, perhaps taking your box with it!

Another useful piece of equipment for the pole angler is a roller. This looks like a painter and decorator's paint roller – only for painting round corners, as it is really two rollers at right angles fixed to the top of a bankstick. Many of the country's best pole anglers swear by a roller, especially when the bank behind them is awkward. So what does a roller do? It makes catching a

The presence of cables is often signposted but check nevertheless.

fish much easier, and losing a fish much more difficult. Hook a good-sized fish using a long pole, or any fish for that matter, and it can easily be lost during the unshipping process as you push the pole back behind you. The butt hits the ground, the resulting bounce shakes the tip of the pole, and the fish falls off. The properly used pole roller prevents this happening, as the butt of the pole is laid in the V of the rest and then pushed back. The rest takes any bounce out of the unshipping process. Sounds easy, and it is. However, make sure the rest is positioned properly, so that after you have unshipped the pole and pulled the sections apart to lift or net your catch, the butt part doesn't lift up into the air out of reach when it's time to push the pole out again. This happens when the part of the pole behind the rest weighs more that the part in front of it, so you might need to make a few adjustments before you're happy. There is, however, a way to stop the butt sections lifting away out of reach, and that's by strategically placing your keepnet so that the front end of the unshipped part can be wedged just under the top ring with the rest placed far enough back to avoid too much pole behind it. Practise this technique and you will eventually reach a happy medium.

Apart from the simple V-type pole rest, others are available that are used with two banksticks and give the angler more space on which to rest his pole. These have two vertical end pieces to stop the pole falling off, with a horizontal roller in between them. Do not, however, assume that you should always use a pole roller when unshipping. Flat, even banks can be handled perfectly well without one, while your rod holdall can also often do the job for you. In fact there are some anglers who never use one at all – it's all down to personal preference.

Cables

There is no greater danger to the pole angler than electricity cables. Carbon fibre, for all its excellent qualities, is also a good conductor of electricity. Touch an overhead cable with a carbon pole and at best you'll be badly burned, at worst you'll be dead. It's a tragic fact that every season the angling press has tales of anglers killed or injured in these circumstances. And it's

Plumbing the depth is important if you are to enjoy pole action like this.

not just overhead cables either. Flat canal or riverbanks are easy places to erect cables, so beware of those running at the back of the path parallel to the water's edge as well. Some of the most innocuous-looking cables are the most dangerous – it's not just large pylons that kill. The simple answer is: do not fish anywhere near cables – there should be warning signs, but even so it is best to check for yourself. You have been warned.

Plumbing the depth

Finding the depth of a swim is one of the most important things you have to discover if you are to enjoy a successful day's fishing, whether floatfishing with a rod and reel, legering or polefishing. The contours of the bottom often provide natural fish-holding areas, which can only be discovered by careful plumbing. You might be using the right rig, right bait and right hook, but if you're fishing in the wrong place, what's the point? You might catch, but what would you have caught if you'd fished in the right place?

Fortunately, plumbing the depth is easy to master and done correctly, it can quickly give you a good idea of what is under the surface.

First, attach your rig to the end of the pole. At this point you will have to estimate the depth, just to give you an idea of the length of line to use – remember what we said about line lengths in the previous chapter. Next, tie your hooklength on to your rig and attach a plummet. There are several types of plummet available. Which you choose is largely down to personal preference, but a few points are worth remembering before making your selection. The best plummets are cork, clip-on or special match plummets.

The traditional plummet has a weight and cork. The hook is threaded through the loop at the top and pushed into the cork. This plummet is good for hooks larger than a size 16 and line stronger than 2 lb breaking strain, but it can damage small hooks and fine lines. It is available in weights of ⅜ oz to 1 oz.

The clip-on plummet originated on the Continent and is designed to clip on to a hook or on to a split shot. It is the only plummet that can be used to clip on to a shot fixed above the hook. If you want to fish with 8 in of line on the bottom, fix a No.4 8 in from the hook, clip the plummet on to this, and you will get an accurate reading. Like the cork plummet, the clip-on plummet can damage fine lines if its spring is too highly tensioned. Available in weights of ¼ oz to 1 oz, the clip-on plummet should be oiled occasionally to prevent rusting.

Recently introduced, the match plummets are, perhaps, the best plummets as they cannot damage small hooks and fine line. A wire loop at the top of the brass plummet is designed to take a hook, which is then secured by a small silicone sleeve. Available in weights of 5 gm, 10 gm and 15 gm. Use the heaviest plummet in the deepest swims.

If you find yourself without a proper plummet, a split shot will suffice. In fact, some anglers prefer nothing more than a simple SSG or AAA split shot as a plummet. Quick and easy, a split shot can be fixed on to the line and removed in seconds. They are not really heavy enough for use on flowing water, however, and split shot can damage fine lines.

Don't always assume you should use the heaviest

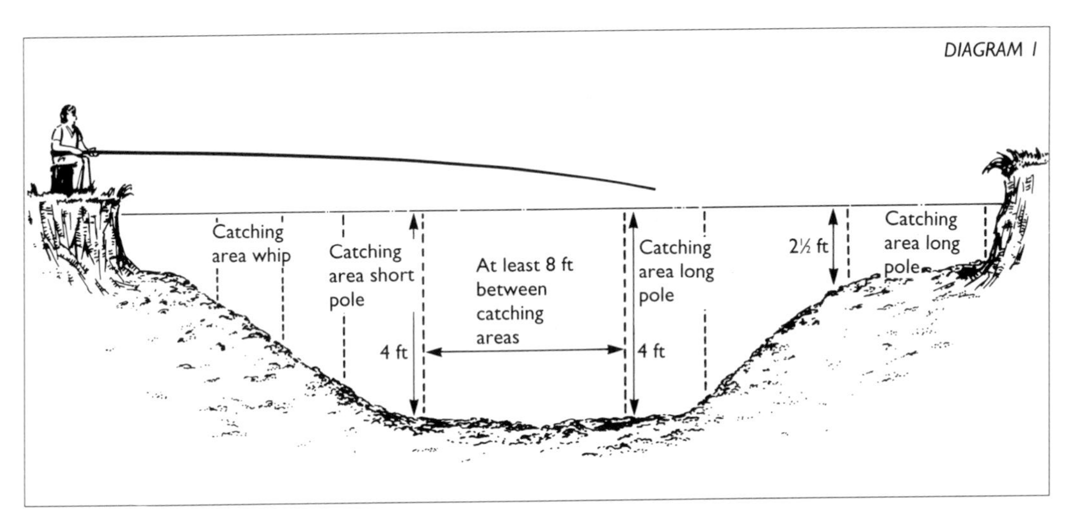

Careful plumbing has revealed no fewer than four swims for this canal pole angler to fish.

plummet when trying to discover the depth. Although a heavy plummet is undoubtedly the easiest from which to obtain a reading – you can feel it hit the bottom and see your pole elastic pull out slightly from the pole-tip when lifting it away – it can also give you a false reading. If the bottom is covered in silt or soft mud, as is often the case on canals, a heavy plummet might sink several inches into it, giving a false reading of the actual depth of the swim. In these circumstances, it would be better to use a lighter one.

The best way to plumb the depth when polefishing is to plumb at what you consider will be the furthest extent of your fishing, and work back towards the near bank by removing one section at a time. By doing this, you will create a mental picture of the underwater contours of your swim. Lower your tackle and plummet carefully and slowly on to your desired plumbing spot, keeping a tight line between pole-tip and plummet, and watch carefully – three things can happen:

The float disappears from view and does not resurface – your tackle is set too shallow. Deepen off by unshipping, retrieving your tackle and moving the float up the line.

The float is left up in the air, above the surface. If the pole is lowered to create slack line, it might even lie on the surface. Shallow up by unshipping, retrieving your tackle, and moving the float down the line. You'll know roughly how far it needs to go by how much line there is between the water surface and your float.

The float tip is just visible at the surface – the tackle is set at the water depth.

Right: after plumbing mark the depth on your pole.

Far right: two types of plummet: clip-on and match.

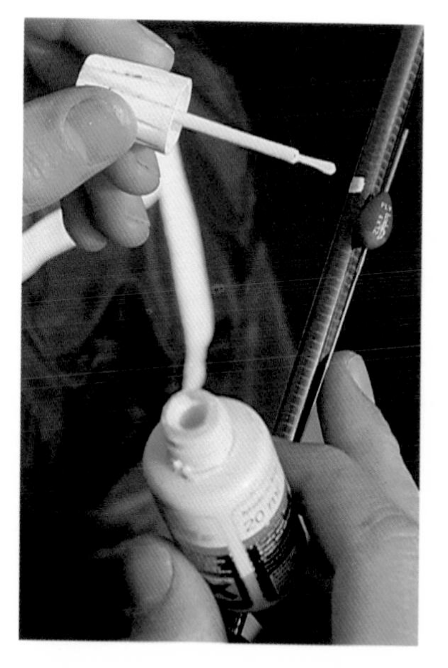

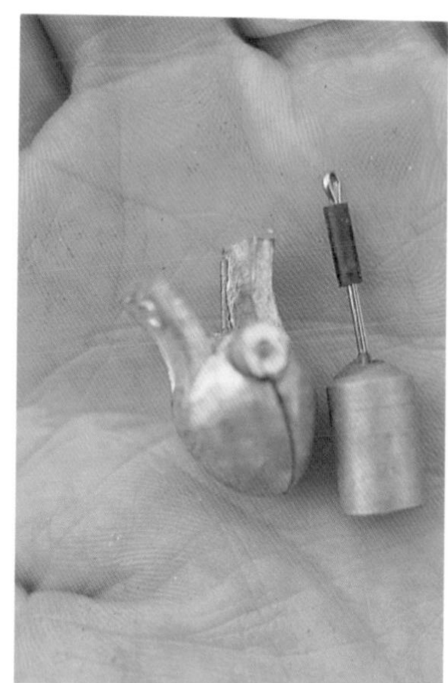

By repeating this process at regular distances, it is possible to get a clear and accurate picture of your swim. And while you are plumbing the depth, try to feel the reaction of the plummet on the bottom. If there's some resistance when you pull the float upwards, the bottom is probably mud or silt. If you feel it scraping over a surface, it could be gravel. A weedy bottom will be easy to spot as you will almost certainly have some weed on your hook and plummet when you retrieve. Use the plummet, then, not only to discover the depth, but also to find a clear spot in between weedbeds.

Plumb carefully lifting and dropping the tackle in several different places.

A pole rest is useful when feeding.

Once you have found the depth, you might want to fish with a few inches of line on the bottom, or a few inches off the bottom. With the float set at the exact depth, that's easy. Move it up or down as required, but not before you know that you can quickly move the float back again to its first setting. There are two ways in which you can know exactly where the float should be positioned to achieve the right setting. The first is to line the tackle up alongside the pole (however many sections coincide with the rig you're using) by slipping your hook under the bottom of the relevant joint. Next, take some typewriter correcting fluid and make a small mark with it on your pole at the place which lines up against the top of the float. The fluid dries in seconds and can be scratched off after the session. The alternative is to mark the line immediately above the float – a thick, black, waterproof marker pen is best for this. Whichever way you choose, you will be certain that you can always move your float back so that your tackle is set at the perfect depth – it provides the base for your whole session.

Holding a pole

A short pole or whip can be easily held with one hand. However, when it comes to wielding 11 m of carbon fibre, it's a different ball-game altogether – and it has to be said that this very basic aspect of polefishing puts many anglers off taking it up in the first place. There is really nothing to it, however, and a little practice will soon see you holding the pole like a world champion.

As in many aspects of the sport, there is never one answer to a problem – several different ways can be employed to hold a long pole. The first way, and the one most easily mastered by beginners, is to grasp the pole right at the butt with one hand (right hand for right-handed anglers) reaching behind, while holding it with the other hand (left hand for right-handed anglers) resting on one knee. The upper leg is used as a rest for the pole.

Perfect, comfortable control can be achieved by holding a pole in this way, but as you become more proficient, you will probably want to hold the pole with both hands close together. Again, the butt section rests on the upper right leg. This method of holding a long pole is favoured in calm weather conditions and works well with lighter poles. It is also conducive to making a clean strike when a bite occurs.

Another way of holding a long pole is to wedge it under and between your legs, leaning out from your box and supporting the butt section with both hands. This is good in a wind, but a little cumbersome, especially after a fish is hooked as you have to move

Two ways of holding a long pole.

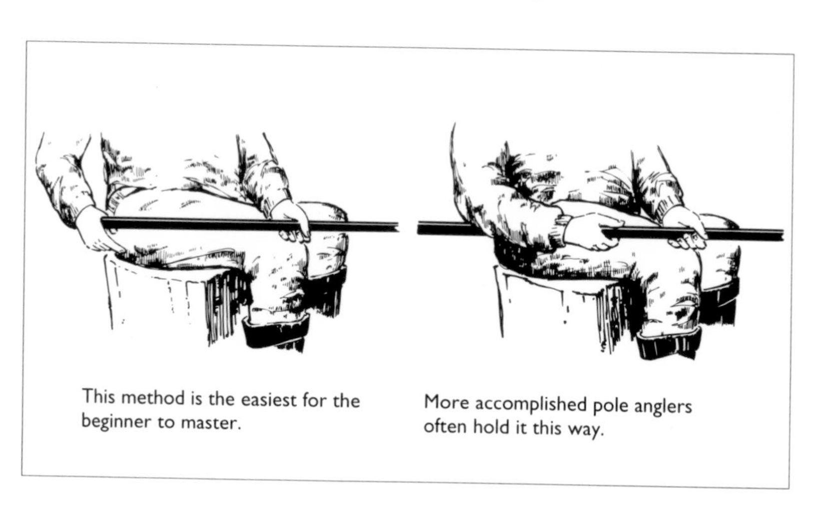

This method is the easiest for the beginner to master.

More accomplished pole anglers often hold it this way.

the pole around in front of your body before you can begin to unship it.

Finally, highly proficient pole anglers and those with expensive, lightweight poles sometimes fish with just one hand holding the pole, grasping the butt section, while supporting it on the upper leg. Again this is something for the expert.

Standing up to use a long pole is not something for the beginner, although as you become more proficient in polefishing the techniques required will gradually become second nature. Even so, it is only really advisable to stand to polefish when fishing with long rigs and highly specialised whips or long poles, such as 'to-hand' fishing on the fish-packed lakes and rivers of Ireland and Denmark.

As you can see, holding a long pole is one of the first disciplines for the would-be pole angler to master. It is best done not only seated, but seated on the level. This is where platforms and box legs come in handy. Although the purchase of a platform might seem a little excessive to the pleasure pole angler, there really is no excuse for not investing in a set of box legs. It takes just a few minutes to attach these to a box, drilling holes in the box according to the manufacturer's instructions and attaching the legs. They might add a little weight to the box, but their advantages far outweigh this small matter. Once on the bankside, all you have to do is spend a couple minutes adjusting each leg so that you end up sitting comfortably, not having to worry about balancing on the edge of the box or perched in such a way that holding the pole is the last thing on your mind.

If you do decide on a platform, you will soon wonder how you ever got by without one. Not only can you use it to place your box on in the shallow margins of a river, drain or canal; even if you don't need it for your box, you can set it up alongside you as a platform for your bait and tackle sundries. It goes without saying that care should be taken when erecting a platform in the margins. It's best to make this your first job when you reach the bankside, setting it up and then leaving it for a good 15 minutes before sitting on it on your box – you will probably find that you can tighten the four legs still more. Extra-wide feet for the legs will help prevent them sinking into soft mud or silt.

Many anglers like to use a pole roller when unshipping.

Tackle layout

A comfortable pole angler is also an effective one, and excessive movement during a session does nothing for your concentration or the feeling of security which your stealthy approach should have instilled in the fish. For this reason, it is vitally important to have everything to hand when you are fishing so that you don't have to keep reaching around for items. A tray for your bait-boxes is extremely useful when it is arranged so that your bait is at waist height. This is especially important for pole anglers, as reaching down while fishing can result in the pole-tip splashing into the water – a recipe for disaster on a shallow canal. Some seat boxes come complete with trays that clip on to the sides. Other excellent trays are available separately, which can be used in conjunction with a bankstick or special box attachment. If you will be groundbaiting regularly, you might need a couple of trays, one on the left for hookbait and loose-feed (if you're right-handed) and one on the right for groundbait.

Another item that needs to be well placed close to hand is your landing-net. One landing-net might seem very much like another, but there are landing-nets tailor-made for polefishing – many canal pole anglers use them. These nets are much smaller, with shorter handles, than those used for other forms of fishing, and are mostly used on shallow waters where the quarry is mainly small fish. They are designed to net quickly anything a little larger than the norm – a 2 oz, soft-mouthed skimmer bream among a run of tiny roach and gudgeon, for example. Many match anglers use them, claiming that the extra few seconds it takes to net a 'borderline' fish can make all the difference at the end of five hours. Of course, they still have their usual landing-net set up as well for anything much bigger, although, again, this might be on a shorter-than-usual handle. Many landing-net handles are just too long for pole swims, which are very shallow with a very short line being used – by the time you have unshipped your pole, the fish is too close to the bank to be netted easily with the handle at full length.

Above: box legs are an alternative to a platform.

Left: well-organised tackle is important when polefishing.

CHAPTER 7

BAITS

You won't get very far in your quest to become the perfect polefisher without baits, and there are numerous different varieties that can be used, just as for rod-and-reel fishing. In fact the only commonly used bait in the coarse angler's armoury that should not be considered when fishing a pole are boilies, although some enterprising carp angler has probably tried a small boilie with pole tackle to reach an otherwise inaccessible under-tree swim! Disregarding these exceptions, however, let us take a look at some of the baits that are widely used and available to the pole angler.

Maggots

Maggots have been the most popular of all baits for years and they will probably remain so for many years to come. They are readily available, easy to look after, and cheap. They are perfect for polefishing in their various shapes, forms and colours, and the type you should use is determined by several factors – most importantly, the size of fish you expect, or hope, to catch. There is no point, for example, fishing with a big hook maggot on a tricky canal swim when you know you'll be catching mainly small roach, gudgeon and perch. A pinkie, or even a squatt, would do a much better job here.

The commonest and most popular type of maggot is the hook maggot – the large, active larva of the bluebottle fly. This maggot is used in thousands of gallons on almost every water in Britain, and it is not surprising to see why. The humble hooker tempts just about every species of coarse fish from bleak to pike. Bites are almost guaranteed, but even so, the hook maggot is best used when conditions are not too hard. They score well on rivers and are much used by pole anglers who want their loose offerings to sink fairly quickly down to the bottom within the confines of their swim, instead of drifting downstream in the current where they – and the fish they attract – will be out of reach of the pole angler's tackle. They are introduced into a pole angler's swim mainly as loose offerings, thrown or with a catapult, but be sparing unless you are certain that you will catch a lot of fish. You can usually tell when there are lots of fish, especially chub, in front of you. Take a look into the mouth of the first one you catch – if it's full of your maggots, there are probably not many more fish out there, so ease off on the loose feed.

When hooking maggots, look for the two tiny 'eyes' in the blunt, rear end of the maggot. By squeezing the bait gently you will see a small piece of skin protrude from between and just below them. This is where you should nick your hook, pushing the point through carefully so that the bait isn't punctured. If a blob of thick, coloured liquid appears as you try to hook the bait, your hook is blunt and needs changing. Use a single maggot on hook sizes from 24 to 20, double on sizes between 20 and 16.

Look for the freshest hookers – or any maggots for that matter – you can find when buying them from the shop. You can tell roughly how fresh they are by the size of the dark patch – called the 'feed spot' – inside the bait. Soon after the maggots have left the meat on which they were bred, this spot is large, filling up more than half the inside. It soon shrinks, however, and a

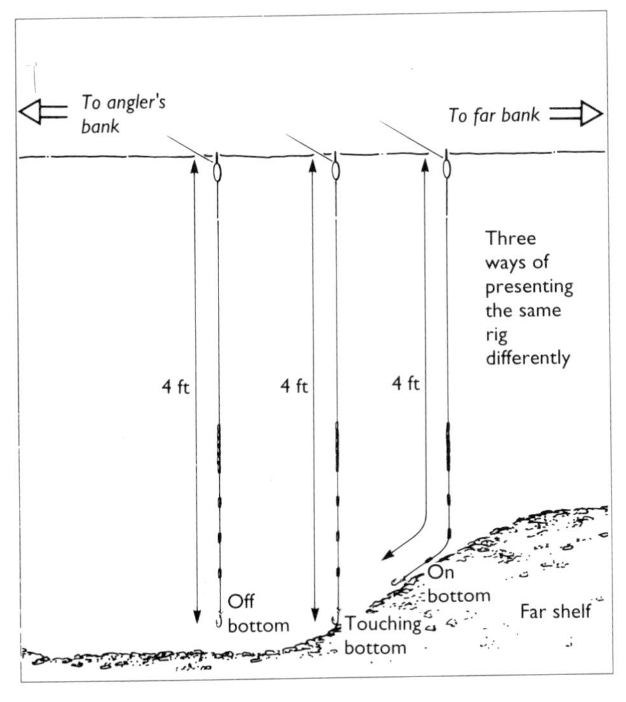

The same bait can be presented to fish in several different ways simply by moving the tackle in or out.

Maggots casters hempseed and a sparkling pole-caught canal roach.

couple of days later the spot will be much smaller. The maggot will also have shrunk a little and its skin will have toughened up as well. Don't worry about this – the bait will be perfect. Just look for the biggest hookers you can find and you won't go far wrong. They are available either in natural white, or in a variety of colours from pink right through to deep bronze. Make sure if you're using coloured maggots that they have been dyed with dyes which are safe for humans. Some maggot dyes were found several years ago to be possible causes of cancer. Stick to the safest dyes, such as the orange food colouring and flavouring turmeric.

If it's clear that big, lively hook maggots are just too large for the fish in front of you, try pinkies. These are the larvae of the smaller greenbottle fly, and are an altogether slimmer maggot than the hooker. Despite their name, pinkies are white when they first are taken off the meat. They turn pink after a couple of days, and this is their likely colour when you buy them from the shop. In some weeks, the pinkies you buy will be much larger than those you buy in other weeks. This is not really important but remember that a large pinkie is best for use as hookbait, while smaller ones could be better for feed.

They are an excellent bait both for feed and on the

hook and can be used as loose feed or in groundbait, although their highly active nature means that it is dangerous to add too many to groundbait – they will soon break up your balls. They are also light and sink slowly, so don't loose feed them in flowing water.

Just like hook maggots, pinkies are available in a variety of colours. Roach seem to like bronze and fluorescent red pinkies, while for bottom-feeding species, red pinkies can be your best bet. Hook them in the same way as you would a maggot, and use size 26 to 22 for a single pinkie, and size 22 to 18 for a double.

One of the best baits of all in the small-water pole angler's armoury is the squatt. This, the smallest maggot, is the larva of the common house fly, and it is very different from its larger cousins, the hooker and the pinkie. Both as feed and hookbait, squatts can be deadly for the pole angler. They are often used on canals (especially those where bloodworm is banned) and drains where regular loose feed and occasional groundbaiting draws a lot of small fish into the area, which are then caught with a single squatt on a small hook and light pole tackle. Some pole anglers specialize in this sort of fishing, and some quite remarkable match catches have been taken on squatts – 10 lb of ½ oz roach is not uncommon. As hookbait, squatts should be used singly on a size 26 to 22 fine-wire hook, or in double or multiples on sizes up to 18. Squatts are also much used as a feed for bream, and if these fish come within range of the pole, the pole can often be the best method of catching them. The best way is to introduce the squatts in a groundbait mix, which will go straight to the bottom, then polefish with a different bait in the same spot. The advantage of squatts is that, unlike

Below left: make maggots float for hookbait by adding a little water to them.

Below: loosefed casters can be a good way to attract roach.

pinkies and hook maggots, they don't tend to burrow into the bottom and disappear. Most will remain visible to a passing shoal.

The two most common colours are natural white and red, although some anglers dye their squatts bronze. They are supplied in red foundry sand, which should be fresh and feel very slightly damp to the touch. Make sure this sand stays a little on the damp side or your bait will float, especially in warm weather. Finally, squatts do not keep very well, so only buy those you expect to use for your next session. Pinkies and hookers, on the other hand, can be kept for a week or more in a cold environment such as a second-hand refrigerator in the garage.

Casters

There's nothing quite like catching fish on the pole with casters. When the float goes under with a caster on the hook, you know there is usually something decent on the other end. It might be a small roach or gudgeon, but more often than not it will be a bigger roach, perch, bream, tench, chub or carp. Many a canal competition has been won by an angler trying caster 'in desperation' in the last hour with pole tackle under a far-side bush. He has one bite, and after a frantic tussle lands a 3 lb carp that pulls him from nowhere to first in the space of a few minutes. They can work just as well on rivers and lakes too, and it's a foolish angler who doesn't take ½ pt with him when he embarks on a polefishing session. Remember that you will need to order them from your tackle shop several days in advance to give your dealer time to prepare them.

Casters are the chrysalis stage of the fly – that part of its life cycle between maggot and fly when the grub stops moving and its soft skin turns crisp, darkening while changes take place inside. Their value as an angler's bait was realized around only 30 years ago, when it was discovered that there is a period of time when casters sink. That's when this bait is deadly. Caster fishing on canals demands the biggest and best bait available; uniform in size and colour and crisp so that a hook point can be pushed easily inside the bait without it squashing or bursting.

When hooking casters, try to bury the hook so that no

part of it is showing, and the best type of hook to use is one made from fine-gauge wire with a wide, round bend. This type of hook will fill a lot of the bait, and your chances of connecting with a fish after it has taken it are very high. All species like casters, and on most occasions they are best fished with several inches of line on the bottom. Casters don't move naturally, so a still bait is what's required here. An exception to this – there's always one – is when fishing a prolific small-carp venue. Here, regular loosefeeding of casters will often prompt the fish to come up in the water to intercept the bait before it reaches the bottom. This is when a caster fished shallow, or even a floating caster that sinks very slowly thanks to the weight of the hook, often succeeds.

Punched bread

One bait that has really caught on among pole anglers in recent years in punched bread. Where large pieces of breadflake and crust have no real place in polefishing, smaller pieces 'punched' from a thick slice of white bread can be a highly successful method of catching roach and skimmer bream. It works particularly well on small, shallow waters when the water is clear, and comes into its own in winter when other baits, like pinkies and squatts, can be unproductive. Punched bread is a delicate bait, well suited to the advantages offered by polefishing with tiny floats and small hooks, and there are a few ways to get even more from this popular method. First, take care with the punch that you use.

A breadpunch is a special angling implement that is pushed into a slice of bread on a hard surface to remove a tiny piece of the slice. The hook point is then pushed into the piece in the punch and the bait removed. Many anglers unused to punched-bread fishing have no confidence that the bait remains on the hook long enough for a fish to take it, but as long as the bread is fresh you should have no problems. One way to ensure it stays on the hook, however, is to take enough slices for a session – three should last you – and cut the crusts off before carefully steaming them for 30 seconds on each side over hot water.

The easiest way of doing this is to pour a little boiling water into a grill-pan, place the pan on a cooker ring set

Above: liquidised bread is good for clear-water roach.

Above right: bloodworm are often the match angler's saviour.

so that the water only just keeps boiling, and use tongs to place slices on to the grid just above the water. Once the slices are steamed, use a rolling-pin to flatten them, and place them individually in small plastic freezer-bags. Once on the bankside, each slice should be removed only when you want to use it. This method of preparing bread for use on the hook produces small pieces that won't swell too much once in the water, but there are days when a more fluffy bait works better. Your best bet is to take a couple of slices of steamed bread and a couple of slices of unsteamed bread from the middle part of a fresh loaf. Then you can experiment.

Nor is the rest of the loaf wasted – this can be used for feed! Cut the crusts off all the slices, feed these (and the two ends) to the birds, and pop the others into the liquidizer. Whizz them around for a minute or two until you're left with fine, fresh breadcrumbs. This is the liquidized bread feed that used to be one of the best-kept secrets of punch fishing. To make it even better, push the liquidized bread through a maggot riddle just before fishing. This bread feed will squeeze together well enough for accurate throwing at distances up to around 10 m – another reason why punched bread and polefishing go hand in hand. The liquidized bread, once in the water, quickly disperses to form at attractive, enticing cloud that the fish will find difficult to resist. All you have to do is present your bait in among this cloud – simple, isn't it? Make sure you carry breadpunches of several different sizes, then you can experiment until you find the one that produces the most fish. The best ones are made from metal, with a slit along the side

Above left: use the largest hemp you can find.

Above: perfectly-mixed groundbait should contain no lumps.

through which you can pull the hook point safely without fear of blunting it along the inside edge of the punch. One final tip: liquidized bread can be filling so don't overdo the feeding. Many anglers like to introduce a small ball of liquidized bread at the start of the session, adding more if bites start to dry up.

Bloodworm and jokers

These two highly specialized baits are best avoided by the beginner to polefishing, although there is no doubt that at times they can be the only baits that will catch fish. They are almost exclusively the domain of the match angler, sometimes difficult to obtain and expensive. In fact, bloodworm and jokers are banned from many venues up and down the country. They are so good that tiny fish often take them, and it is felt that the capture of these immature fish can damage a fishery in the future. If you do fancy giving them a try, you will need to order them well in advance, and even then your tackle dealer might not be able to oblige.

Both are larvae of different types of midge, and the normal way of using them is to feed with jokers while using bloodworm on the hook. The jokers should be fed either in groundbait or 'neat', with only a sprinkling of special clay to give them enough weight to be thrown into a swim. The bloodworm is then fished on a small, fine-wire hook like a size 24, with the bait just touching the bottom. It can be a deadly method on difficult canals – and again the delicacy of presentation offered by polefishing is perfectly suited to the task.

Hempseed

Anyone who has never experienced a good day 'on the hemp' has missed out on one of the most enjoyable of all polefishing experiences. Hempseed is anything but an instant bait, but once bites do come, the action can be fast and furious. The seed of a plant, hemp has to be cooked before it can be used as an angler's bait. To do this, soak 1 pt or so in plenty of water overnight, then rinse in a sieve, add more water and bring to the boil on the top of the stove. Now turn the heat down a little so that the water carries on boiling. After half an hour or so you should have dark-coloured seeds, many of which have split to reveal the white insides. A teaspoon of sodium bicarbonate added to the water before it boils will make the seeds go even darker. Once they're cooked, rinse them again in cold water and place in a bait-box.

Hempseed can be used as loose feed with maggot fished over the top, or it can be fished on the hook itself. It takes a little practice to hook a grain of hemp, but as long as the right grain is selected – choose one that is barely split – you should be able to manage it in a second or two by pushing the bend of the hook into the split between the two sides of the grain kernel. Never give up on hempseed. Even if you're catching on maggot while feeding hemp, every now and then try a grain of hemp on the hook. Eventually the float will dip and you should immediately see the size of your fish increase. Roach are suckers for it, and polefishing is undoubtedly the best way to use it as bites have to be hit quickly. Use a size 18 hook and shot the float with a small 'bulk' of an olivette or styl weights at just below mid-depth. Under that should go enough styl weights at 6-in intervals down to 6 in above the hook. Don't use round split shot when hemp fishing. Fish will mistake them for hemp, and false 'shot' bites will result. Try cooked tares as well – these are larger than hempseed and fewer bites will be missed with these on the hook.

Groundbait

On most occasions it would be wise to take some groundbait with you when polefishing. Whether you use it or not depends on the venue you are fishing and just

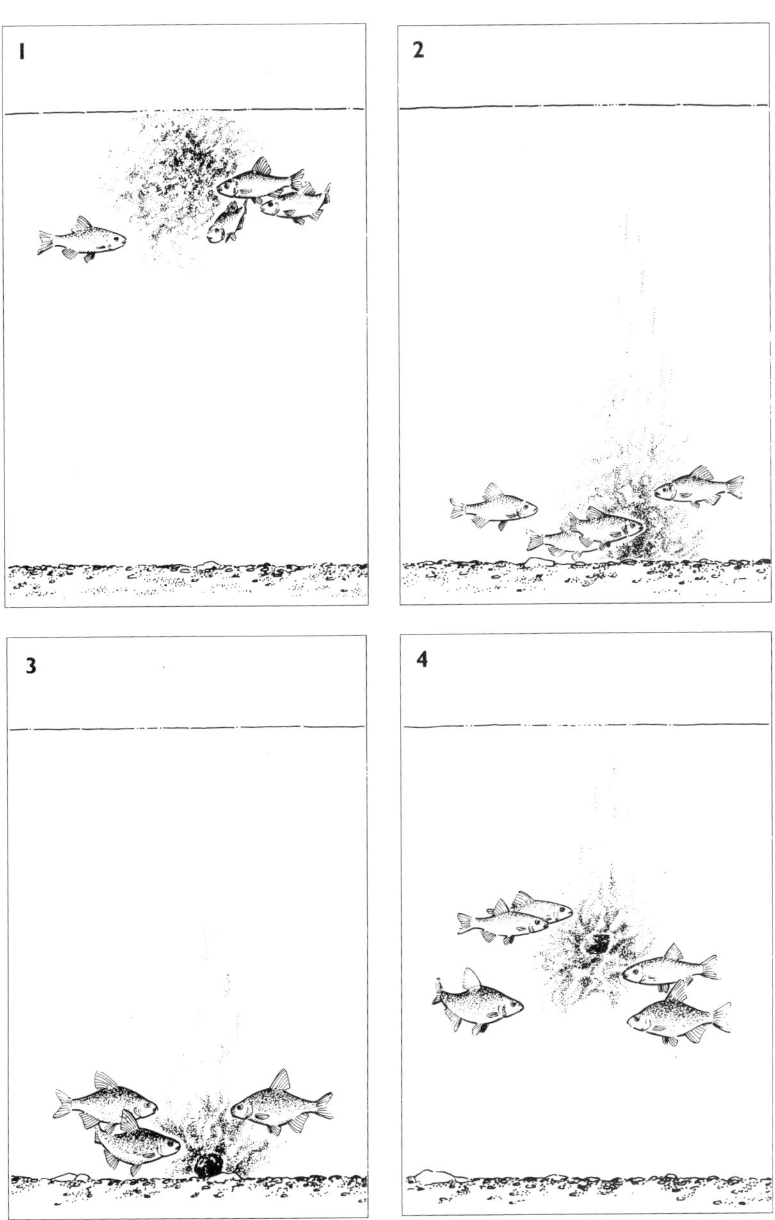

Different consistencies of groundbait work in different ways.

1: Cloud groundbait breaks at the surface.

2: Slop disperses from the bottom.

3: Heavy groundbait can take a long time to break up.

4: Fluffy groundbait disperses on its way down.

how the fish are reacting. If you are fishing for roach and chub on a river, for example, you probably won't need it – loose-fed maggots should do the trick here. If a shoal of bream arrive in the swim, however, a few balls of groundbait wouldn't go amiss. It really comes into its own, however, when you want to catch large numbers of fish in smaller waters. Here, a small ball of carefully mixed groundbait can result in a bite every cast if pinkies or squatts are loosefed sparingly over the top.

The proportions of groundbait and loose feed should be determined by how the fish are feeding on the day – sometimes they will want more groundbait than loose feed, sometimes it is the other way round. For shallow waters, don't bother adding any 'meat', like squatts or pinkies, to your groundbait. Loosefeeding should be adequate, along with a fine groundbait mixed with only a minimum of water so that it can only just be squeezed into a ball and breaks up on impact with the water. For this sort of fishing, use a small pole float with a 'strung-out' rig of styl weights or shot, and expect bites at all levels in the water. Feed a tiny ball of groundbait every cast.

In deeper swims with fish feeding closer to the bottom, a heavier groundbait mix is required that will not break up immediately, but which will start to disperse at it approaches the bottom. A few hookbait samples should be added to the feed, and a pole rig used that contains a 'bulk' in the form of several shot, styls or an olivette, followed by one or more 'droppers' between this and the hook. Remember to mix your groundbait carefully, removing any lumps by pushing it through a maggot riddle.

London angler Glenn Brown used maggots fished on a pole for this fine fine catch of bream.

CHAPTER EIGHT

YOUR FIRST BITE

Everything is ready. You've found an attractive swim and you've decided to fish with all but one section of your 11-m pole. The swim itself is 4 ft deep and hardly moving, so you plump for a rig whose length corresponds to the top four sections of your pole. How do you get your tackle into the water? Although this might seem hardly worth mentioning to accomplished pole anglers, the simple act of 'casting' with a pole can be a daunting prospect for the beginner.

Step 1

With the length of your pole corresponding to the length of the rig in your right hand, and holding your line just above the baited hook in your left, pull the line

Kent tackle dealer Charlie Lovell starts to push his tackle out to the water.

a little to check that the elastic is flowing freely. If it is not, it's tangled and needs looking at. If it pulls out but in a series of jerks, it needs treating with some elastic lubricant. If everything is fine, flick the tackle overarm into the margins, making sure that it doesn't land on any weed and that your hook doesn't end up fouling your keep-net.

Step 2

Assemble the rest of your pole except for the butt section, ideally going away behind you with the front end of the fifth section wedged into the top ring of your keepnet or simply lying on the ground if the bank is flat. Take this front end and push it into the rear end of the fourth section.

Step 3

Now comes the process known as 'shipping'. This involves carefully pushing the pole and tackle out into the water between both arms until the whole of the pole you intend to use is out in the swim and you're holding on to the butt section.

Step 4

During the shipping process, make sure that the pole-tip doesn't become tangled with the line, and try to keep the float and rig in the water, ensuring that the pole-tip doesn't bounce, which usually has the result of wrapping the rig around the pole-tip. Once you have reached the required distance, lift the pole sharply to pull the rig from the water and move it so the tip makes a rough half circle, resulting in the tackle flicking over and landing in a straight line in the water. This action is important and practise it. Not only does it avoid tangles, it makes sure that the bait falls through the water well away from the pole tip and in a natural fashion. Laying out your tackle in a straight line can also be done underarm in favourable wind conditions, but it requires more practice to achieve the correct technique.

Striking and unshipping

When you're using a long pole, every tiny movement of your hands is magnified considerably 10 m away at the pole-tip. For this reason, the strike must be a controlled exercise, totally different from the one you would make if you were fishing at the same distance with rod-and-reel tackle. Watch for every movement of the pole float.

If you've shotted it correctly and just the very tip is showing, it should simply disappear from view under the surface of the water. Perhaps if you're fishing for roach feeding at all levels in the water, the float tip might hold up slightly when a fish intercepts your slowly sinking bait as it falls through the water. It might even start to move slowly against or a little faster than any current. Whatever happens, if you think you've got a bite, you must strike. The best strike to employ when polefishing is slightly to the diagonal, making sure you don't 'hit' the float by striking too much to the side. Similarly, if you strike directly upwards, you might then have to lower the poletip again to allow you to push the pole back behind you without the its butt hitting the ground.

Step 1

This is the real test of a pole angler's preparation. If you have done everything correctly, the strike is met by a few inches of elastic being pulled from the poletip as the impact of the hook penetrating the fish is absorbed, even if it's a small fish. In shallow water, this strike should be a diagonal movement of the pole-tip through a relatively short distance until the resistance of the fish is felt. If the water is deeper, you will probably need to increase the movement. Once you have hooked the fish successfully, you must try to assess its size as quickly as possible before starting to bring it to the bank.

Step 2

Having assessed the size of your fish, you can begin the process known as 'unshipping'. Let's assume it is a small fish. Look behind you and pass the pole through your hands, resting the butt on a smooth surface or in the V of a pole roller, until you reach the joint that leaves the pole length equal to the length of line you are using.

Step 3

Once you have reached the right joint, pull the pole apart. Rest the section of the pole that is behind you so that it won't swing round or up (one way is to wedge the front end of the fifth section in to the mouth of your keepnet – we're using a four-section rig, remember). You must make sure it doesn't slide into the water, something which can be a problem on sloping banks.

Step 4

Check that the fish is still hooked – if you've done everything right, it should be – by watching the elastic

Above: pushing the pole back before unshipping.

Opposite: after unshipping the fish can be swung safely to hand.

from the pole-tip. Take your right hand (now redundant) and swop it with your left so that it now holds your pole, and swing in the fish or net it as required.

Although this sounds a difficult process, with just a little practice you will find it becomes second nature and is one of the most enjoyable of all aspects of polefishing. You can make the job easier still by using hooks that have a small barb, rather than barbless ones. Even if a little slack line is created during the unshipping process, the barb will help prevent the fish from slipping the hook.

Playing larger fish

What happens if the fish you have hooked is much larger than you bargained for? You'll soon know, because the elastic shoots out from the pole-tip as it makes its bid for freedom and heads for the far side. Here is another test of your preparation. Any weak links in hook, knots, line or elastic will be revealed and the fish will be quickly lost. It is a common scenario on canals where the angler is happily catching roach using

casters, and suddenly the swim goes quiet for a few minutes before a carp is hooked.

The first thing is not to panic. With skill and a little luck there is no reason why the fish should not be landed. Pole-elastic is an amazing material and although you have no extra line to give a running fish, elastic can stretch a long way. And as it stretches, its tension increases. This is your major ally when it comes to landing fish. Another good tip is to have the next section of your pole – if there is one – strategically placed behind you so that if you do hook something substantial and it starts to charge away, you can add this section to catch up with the fish. Don't rush things. Hold the pole as still as you can, letting the elastic do the work it's designed for, and be in no rush to start the unshipping process. It's better to let the fish run in open water than give it the chance to dive under the near bank by unshipping too early. Soon the fish should start to tire and you can start unshipping. Usually it is just a case of pushing the pole behind you and pulling it apart at the relevant section. You can still do this with a big fish, but be prepared to push the pole back out again before unshipping if the fish makes a sudden run. Another way with big fish is to unship one section at a time, resting each of the unshipped sections behind you as you go. If you've done everything right, eventually the fish will be beaten on the surface and you can unship fully before netting it.

Netting

With small fish, lifting them from the water simply means unshipping the pole at the right section and swinging them to hand. When it's a case of netting them, however, sometimes you might need to unship at a different section. This all depends on the behaviour of the fish once it reaches the surface. Take chub, for example. They tend to stay still at the surface once they have a mouthful of air, and you can then use the pole and elastic to pull them to the waiting net. The process is made easier if you unship one section fewer than normal so that more elastic is pulled from the pole tip and the fish can be netted. The elastic stretches to put the fish under pressure, but as long as it remains relatively quiet on the surface no losses should occur.

The same process can be employed with bream. For carp and roach, however, you would do better to unship to your usual section with less elastic out from the pole-tip. These fish tend to thrash around on the surface more, and they can easily be lost if the elastic is stretched to put them under considerable pressure.

Feeding

Beginners to polefishing often like to feed by placing the pole in a pole rest attached to the side of their box. By doing this, they have both hands free to throw or catapult groundbait or loose feed to the desired area. However, when it's a case of feeding regularly, it is time-consuming to place the pole in a rest every time, and can waste a lot of time over the course of a session. The answer is to learn how to feed while still holding the pole.

There are several ways in which you can feed without having to place the pole in a rest, and the method you choose should depend on personal preference, the distance to be achieved, wind conditions and whether you are using groundbait or loosefeed. The golden rule before feeding anything is this: always make sure your feed is at pole level. You do not want to be reaching down to the ground every time you want to feed. Trays at roughly the same height as the top of the box will make the job much easier. Let us assume that you want

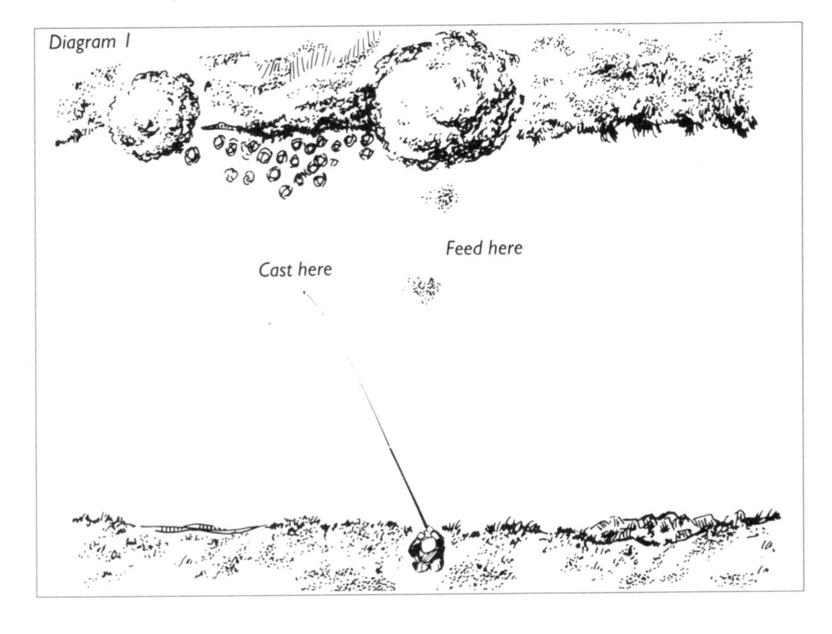

Left: two swims on a canal will allow fish to be caught all day. Make sure you drop your tackle a little downwind of your feed.

Some pole anglers like to feed by leaning over to trap the pole.

to introduce regular helpings of loose feed to your swim, which is 11 m out into a lake. Three methods can be employed with a catapult – throwing loose feed is out of the question at such distances.

Perhaps the best way for the beginner to feed is by wedging the pole butt between his legs. By doing this and crossing his legs, a sort of temporary pole rest is formed and both hands are free to feed.

The second method, affectionately known as the 'beer-gut' method, involves leaning over and feeding by wedging the pole between your foreleg and the bottom of your ribcage or, better still, your stomach. Drinking anglers enjoy a considerable advantage here!

The third method is one practised by the majority of accomplished pole anglers and involves controlling the pole by wedging the butt section between your upper leg and forearm. With the bait at box-lid level to your left and your catapult pouch hanging from your bait-tray, loose feed is dropped into the pouch. The left

Left: it is safest to net any pole-caught fish weighing more than around 3 oz.

Below: large fish can be landed on pole tackle with a little care.

hand then takes the catapult frame and passes it in front of the body so that the right fingers can grasp the pouch while it still maintains its hold on he pole. Bait is then fired into the swim by pulling the frame away from the pouch with the left hand and releasing the pouch. The bait will be propelled along the pole and with practise it will become easy.

This last method, although the best one to use in most conditions as it requires very little movement of the pole, can be difficult when it's windy as the pole is not held as tightly as it might be with the others.

With all three feeding methods, it's important that you are not sitting too high on your box. Some Continental boxes see the angler almost dangling his legs because there are so many trays incorporated into the lid. If you're to feed easily and correctly with a catapult, one or more of these trays will need to be removed and placed to one side before you start to fish.

It is also a good idea, when feeding with a catapult, to use a small one, with a triangular as opposed to a mesh pouch, and short elastic of only 6 in or so. Bait can be dropped inside this type of pouch easily, whereas with a mesh pouch maggots would quickly fall off. And the short elastic minimizes tangles.

If you're in any doubt about these feeding techniques, the simple answer is: don't try them. It doesn't really take very long to unship your pole to feed, or to feed before casting. Especially when you are feeding only occasionally – caster fishing on a canal, for example – there is no point in running the risk of spraying bait all over the river. For regular feeding of maggots, pinkies and squatts, however, it is probably worth the trouble of practising until you get it right.

Groundbaiting can also be carried out while you are holding the pole, by placing the bowl of mixed groundbait at hand height to the right of your box and squeezing and throwing the ball of groundbait with your right hand while wedging the pole butt into your groin and supporting it a little way up the butt section in your left hand. Some anglers prefer to stand while they feed but the process remains the same.

While on the subject of feeding, it is worth pointing out that great care must be taken to ensure that it lands in the desired place. Many's the time a pole angler has missed out on a good catch because he was fishing nowhere hear his feed. There were plenty of fish in front of him, but he was fishing in the wrong place. On a flowing river, it is imperative to feed a little upstream of where you are fishing, and you must make sure that you let the tackle travel far enough down your swim to make the most of that feed – again, you can see the need for a longer line between pole-tip and float on flowing water than you often need on still water. The deeper the water and the faster the flow, the higher up your swim you will need to feed and the further down your swim you will need to let your float travel.

There is another way of allowing your tackle to 'cover' as much of your swim as possible, useful in windy conditions when too much line between pole-tip and float is hindering good bait presentation. That method is to use pole one section longer than you need, but start the trot through the swim by holding the pole so that the extra section is behind you. As the float nears its downstream limit and the line between it and the pole-tip starts to straighten, pass this extra section between your hands to give you extra length in front of your body and the float will be able to travel further.

CHAPTER 9

FISHING THE WHIP

Many beginners to polefishing think it is a good idea to start off by using a whip. While the merits of this are to be questioned, fishing the whip is an extremely enjoyable pastime and a discipline worth acquiring. As long as the fish come within a certain distance from the bank, the whip can be your passport to a big catch. Broadly speaking, whips are telescopic or partly-telescopic poles of between 1 and 10 m in length. Unlike true long poles, where a much shorter length of line is used between pole-tip and hook, fully telescopic whips are fished with line attached to the tip that is the same length as the whip, or slightly shorter. It has to be this way because unshipping cannot be done. No sections of a true whip are taken apart to bring in a hooked fish. It has to be swung straight to hand or brought to the landing-net because it is impossible to remove a telescopic section by unshipping.

Opposite: Jan Porter works with a long whip on the River Trent.

Left: whips are great for fishing close in.

Line can be attached to the end of a whip in several different ways. There are two ways of attaching it using rubber sleeves. Both are shown here and both are equally effective:

METHOD 1

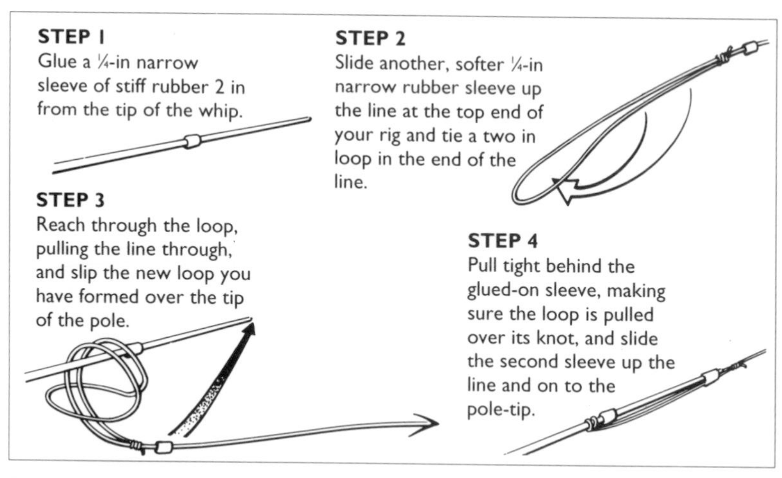

METHOD 2

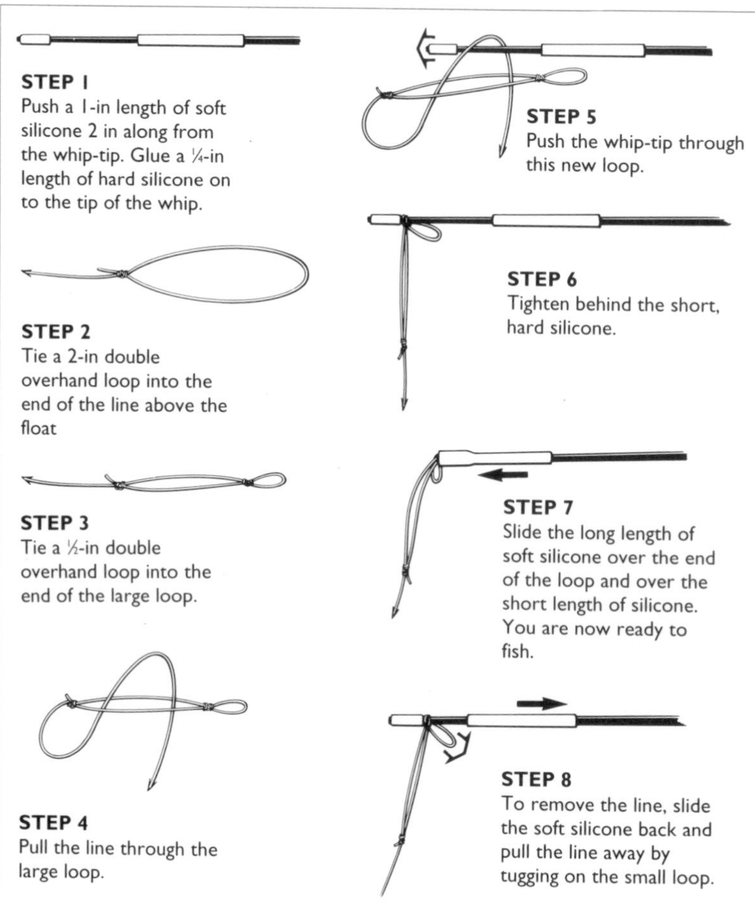

There are other ways of attaching line to the tip of the whip based on these two, while beginners might find it easiest of all is to glue on a special tiny connector available from most good tackle shops. Connectors come in several different sizes, and you would do best to take your whip into the shop and try them for yourself until you find the one that fits the tip tightly. Your tackle dealer will help. These connectors have a movable sleeve, which slides back to reveal a tiny hook. A loop tied into the end of your line is then slipped over the hook before the sleeve is replaced over both hook and loop. Then you're ready.

Lengths

Whips can be obtained in a variety of different lengths, from little more than 1 m to up to 10 m, but a beginner to whip fishing need not bother with either of these two extremes. A whip of 4 or 5 m is the best length to set you on your way. This length will enable you to fish swims of average depth on most rivers, lakes and canals up and down the country.

Obviously, as your whip-fishing prowess grows, you will want to increase your collection, and top match anglers have a dozen or more whips to cater for every possible situation. Do remember, however, that it is more difficult to control your tackle with a longer whip than it is with a shorter one. This is because, unless your swim is very deep, you will have a lot of line between pole tip and float and as this line gets blown about by the wind, the presentation of your end tackle will suffer.

Elastic

The essence of whip fishing is to catch fish quickly, and in most situations this means small fish. It follows, then, that a softish tip at the end of the whip is better than elastic. This soft tip – called a flick-tip – will not cause fish to be 'bumped', whereas elastic can pose this problem with small fish. However, on venues where the occasional larger fish can be expected, elastic is a good insurance against losing them. It is amazing that large fish can often be landed with a whip. Sometimes an unwary tench or big perch will be in the landing-net almost before it realizes it's been hooked!

Good-quality fish can be landed with care on a whip.

Pros and cons

As there is no reeling and casting out involved, you can see why whips are built for speed. Get it right, and it's simply a case of flicking your tackle out, waiting for it to settle, and getting a bite. Then all you have to do is strike and swing the fish straight to your hand. Simple, isn't it? You can be certain you're dropping your tackle into the same place every time, and as long as your feed is fairly accurate too, you can congregate a shoal of small fish just where you want them.

However, with such an efficient way of fishing, there has to be a catch. In the case of the whip, this is the fact that conditions have to be favourable for whips to work properly. If the tackle is cast out straight in front of the angler, any awkward wind will soon 'pick up' the line between whip-tip and float and start to blow the tackle off line. If bites are coming quickly after casting, that shouldn't be a problem, but if you're having to wait a little time, your bait presentation will suffer badly.

Whip fishing isn't totally out of the question if it is windy. You can still catch with a whip, but you might have to change the way in which you use it slightly. If you were using a 4-m whip on a calm day, for example, flicking the tackle overhead, you could be fishing, say, 6 m out. On a windy day, in order to reach the same distance you would be much better off using a longer whip and casting a little downwind. If your tackle settles downwind of the tip of your whip, with 90 degrees between whip-tip and float, control will be much improved and you will still be fishing faster than you would if you had to unship. In this situation, of course, you must remember to feed downwind too, to ensure your feed is in the vicinity of your hookbait when it reaches your fishing spot.

Another way of making a whip work in windy conditions is to use a float attached at the bottom end only, as opposed to a conventional top-and-bottom pole float. With your float attached through the bottom eye only, you can sink your line out of the way of the wind after casting by dipping the tip of the whip under the surface and pulling sharply towards you. You should be able to see the two ends of your line join midway between whip-tip and float. This is a good method to employ if you're trying to catch fish feeding 'on the drop'. Use a small, all-balsa float for this, shotted with most of the float's casting weight used to lock it in place, and just three or four small No.8s or No.10s fixed at equal distances between float and hook.

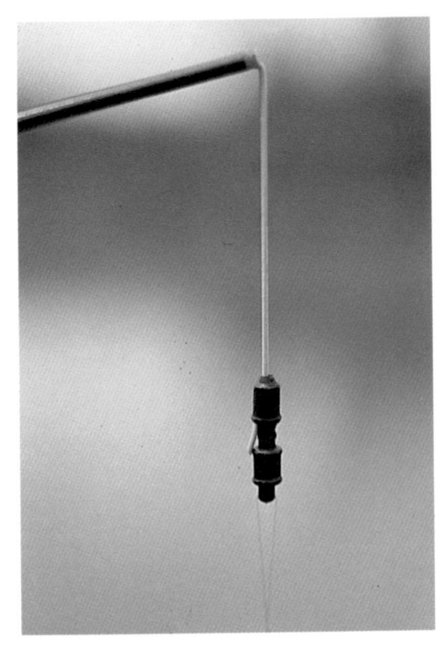

Above: regular feeding with small balls of wet groundbait will keep the fish near the bottom.

Left: elastic can be used with a whip if big fish might be encountered.

In awkward wind conditions use a longer whip and fish downwind.

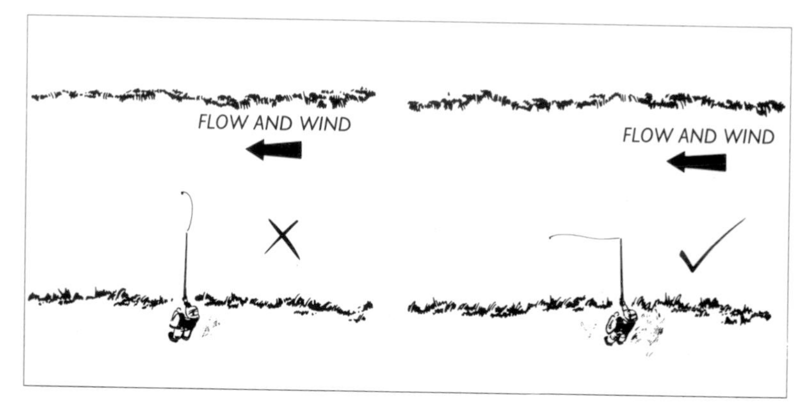

Rigs

Those same rigs we examined earlier will be perfectly adequate for whip fishing, as long as you follow the same rules regarding float shape. One thing to remember, however, is that usually a heavier float will be required for casting a whip than is needed for fishing at the same distance with a long pole and short line. This is because extra casting weight is needed. Cane-stemmed floats are also very good for whip fishing because they move through the air well, whereas occasionally floats with wire stems will twist in mid-air and become tangled.

Feeding

To catch small fish regularly while using a whip, steady feeding on the 'little-and-often' principle is often needed. Groundbait is important and many anglers swear by it as a feed to keep fish in the area. Even if they don't actually eat it, fish will be attracted by a cloudy patch in the water. Often then it's a case of loosefeeding small hookbait samples like squatts and pinkies over the top. Groundbait for fish that are feeding at all levels in the water should be mixed by adding the minimum amount of water so that it holds together only just well enough to be thrown, dispersing immediately it hits the water and perhaps even floating for a couple of seconds before 'exploding' and sinking. Mix it carefully and try to remove all the lumps either by pushing it through a maggot riddle or rubbing it many times between your fingers. Then, by feeding small pieces little larger than your thumbnail, you will create an attractive cloud in the water from the surface downwards. By dropping your hookbait in among the cloud, you should ensure a regular supply of bites.

If, on the other hand, you want to keep the fish near to the bottom, mix your groundbait a lot wetter. 'Slop', as it is called, will sink quickly and cloud once it has hit the bottom. A commercial groundbait with active particles will enhance this process. Choice of groundbait is down to personal preference. Some anglers prefer plain, good-quality brown crumb, while others like to make their own blend from the large range of Continental-type feeds available. However, whichever one you do use, don't add much live feed to groundbait for whip fishing, if any at all. Loosefeed it instead, adding a few samples every time you feed a ball of groundbait. You might find on some days that the fish don't want any loose feed at all, while on others the opposite is the case. The ability to determine what the fish prefer and take the right decisions is what makes an average pole angler into a good one.

Take-apart

As more and more anglers realized the true worth of fishing 'to-hand' with whips, enterprising manufacturers started producing whips that were far more versatile

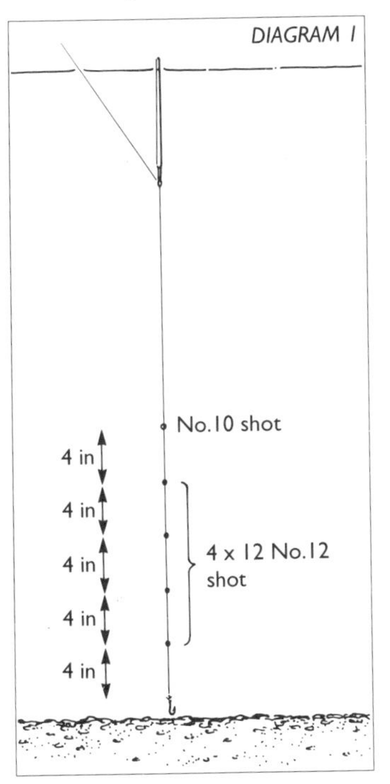

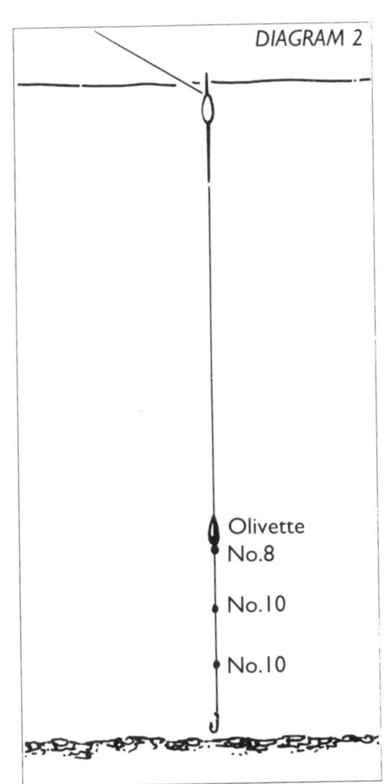

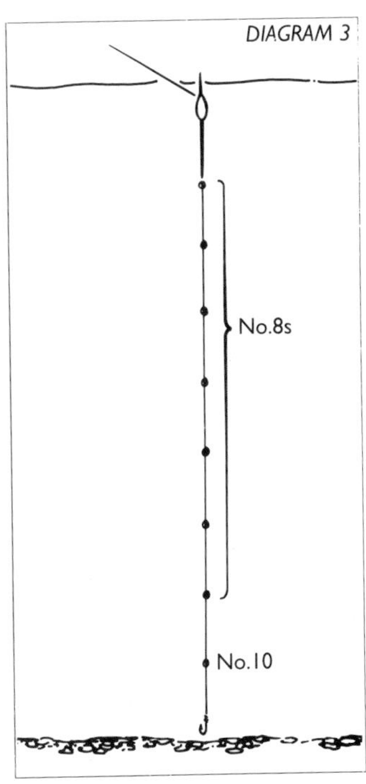

Three rigs for the whip.

Diagram 1: a typical whip waggler rig.

Diagram 2: a rig for bottom-feeding fish.

Diagram 3: a rig for catching on the drop.

than their predecessors, combining telescopic and take-apart sections. On a 6-m whip of this type, for example, the top three sections might be telescopic, the bottom three sections take-apart. The advantages are numerous: the angler can use it as a conventional 'to-hand' whip at 3, 4, 5 or 6 m; you can add on extra sections and extra line if the fish decide to move further out, as often happens on canals and other small waters; and you can use it with three sections worth of line, but add on extra sections if conditions don't allow a 'to-hand' whip to be used successfully.

Casting a long whip is best done with a sideways motion.

Long whips

In recent years a few brave anglers have started to realize the potential of whips that are much longer than those which had previously been used. Matchmen like Jan Porter have, in fact, won some big competitions by using these long whips when most other anglers wouldn't have dreamed of even setting one up. Whips of longer than 7 or 8 m demand a very different technique from shorter whips, but on their day they have many advantages over other, more conventional methods.

First, a long whip is fast – very fast. Hook a small fish on a 10-m whip and it's out of the water and in the net in seconds. Not only is this useful to the match angler for whom speed is of prime importance, it also means that disturbance to the shoal is over in a split second. Next, a strike made with a long whip is much faster than the strike made with a rod-and-reel set-up. There is very little line actually in the water between float and poletip when the strike is made, and consequently, more fish are hooked as there is less resistance on the strike.

Thirdly, the angler fishing a long whip can always be certain he is fishing the same distance out – not always the case when using a rod and reel. And much more of a swim on running water can be 'covered' by fishing 10

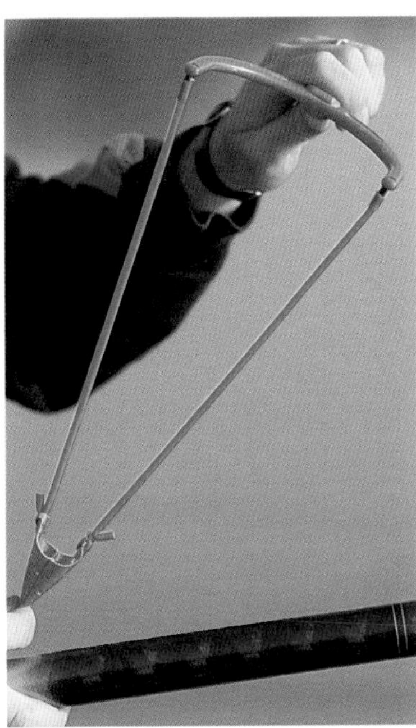

Feeding while standing with a long whip.

Far left: drop the bait in the catapult pouch.

Left: take the catapult round the front of your body and feed by pulling on the frame.

m to hand than it can be using a long pole and short line. This is achieved by following the float down the swim with the tip of the whip, using the full length of line to its maximum potential. And finally, excellent control is possible with a 10-m whip in flowing water as the tip of the whip is directly upstream of the float, following it along the swim in a line almost parallel to the bank. This means than even a light float will not be dragged off line in a downstream wind – a notorious problem with a much shorter rod and stick float or waggler.

However, there's always a catch, and long whips do have their limitations. For a start, any wind will affect a 10-m whip much more than it affects a 13-ft float rod; as with shorter whips, there's not a lot of shock-absorbing qualities in a long whip – unexpected large fish will probably be lost; long-trotting with a stick float can cover more of a swim on a river than using a long whip; distance fished from the bank is limited to a little further than the length of the whip in flowing water (although greater distances can be fished with the same length of whip in stillwaters, where the extra length of line is used for distance out into the lake, not for distance along a flowing swim); and swinging in or landing fish takes considerable skill and technique.

Unlike most shorter whips, long, all-telescopic whips need a lot of flexibility right along their length. Casting, striking and playing fish are all much easier with a long whip that bends all through if you want it to, rather than with one that bends only at the tip.

Considerable skill and practise are needed to use a long whip effectively. Even casting the tackle into the water requires a technique probably very different from anything else you're used to. It is best described in two stages:

Step 1

Holding the whip in your right hand and the line just above the hook in your left, swing the pole to the left to some degrees from the bank. Now swing it back out towards the swim, releasing the line so that the tackle flies out in a straight line.

Step 2

Now watch carefully as the tackle starts its approach to the water. If you're on a river, you will need to control the whip to make sure that the tackle lands in a straight line – no problem if the river is flowing from right to left, but if it's moving from left to right you will probably need to pull the tackle upstream once it has landed so that it runs through the swim correctly. On stillwaters, the tackle can be cast overhead, which means that potentially distances of almost 20 m can be fished with a 10-m whip.

Feeding

Cumbersome to use for the beginner to polefishing, very long whips are best fished standing up, with a bait apron and catapult close at hand so feeding is easily done in four stages:

Step 1
Drop the required amount of loose-feed into the pouch of the catapult, which should be hanging down from your left side, while you hold the long whip in your right hand, wedged into your stomach if need be.

Step 2
Remove the catapult frame from its pouch on your bait apron with your left hand, still holding the whip with your right.

Step 3
Pass the catapult around the front of your body and grasp the pouch between two fingers of your right hand while still holding the whip.

Step 4
Keep the right hand where it is and stretch the elastic by pulling the frame forwards with your left hand. Release the pouch, firing the bait along the pole.

CHAPTER 10

POLE ANSWERS

By now you should have learned most of the basics of polefishing, and it's a question of putting theory into practice and perfecting the techniques described in this book. At first, polefishing will be an alien concept to the angler who has spent most of his fishing life with much shorter rods and reels. However, once you have made the decision to take it up, you will never want to put your pole down!

In this chapter, some of the questions experienced pole anglers are often asked by those new to the sport are answered.

Q What are the best knots to use when polefishing, both for elastic and for line.

A Elastic is funny stuff, and any knots tied into it must be tied very carefully indeed. Once a knot in elastic is properly secured, it will probably outlive the elastic itself. Securing it in the first place is the biggest problem! When tying knots in elastic, the elastic must be perfectly dry – on no account should you treat it with any lubricant before tying it at both ends to various

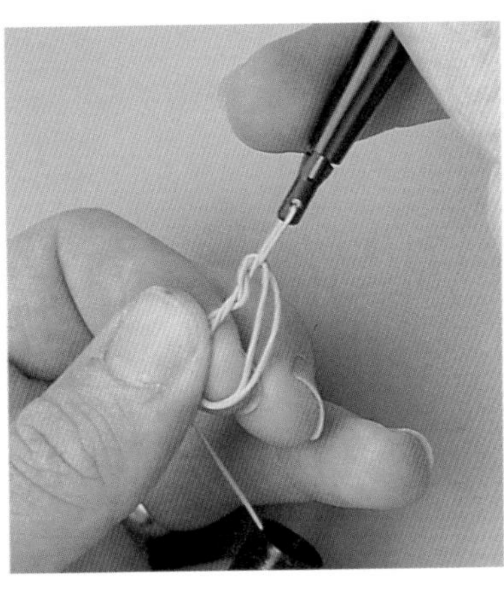

Far left: high-tech lines are good for polefishing but use them with care.

Left: take time in tying knots in elastic.

Opposite: Essex angler Pete Clapperton hooks a good fish from the Great Ouse.

plugs and connectors. If you do have to tie it during the course of a session, when it is wet, dry it as thoroughly as you can with a cloth or the knot will never tighten. The best knot is the simple single overhand loop, tightened properly by stretching the elastic as you pull the knot together. When tight, release the elastic,which should then actually grip on to itself in the knot. If you've done everything right, this single overhand loop should be sufficient, but there's no harm in adding another one or two more – if only for your peace of mind.

Monofilament line is also difficult to tie properly, and sometimes quite specialized knots have to be used. The knot problem has been complicated by the introduction of low-diameter, high-tech lines, which don't respond at all well to certain types of knot.

What is the best knot, for example, for joining main pole line to hooklength? The answer for polefishing is the two-loop knot, where a small loop is tied in the end of the main line and in the end of the hooklength and they are then joined together. This is the knot every would-be pole angler should learn, if he hasn't already done so in his rod-and-reel apprenticeship. The best way of tying the first stage of this knot – the loop itself – can be described in four simple stages.

The Double Overhand Loop

STEP 1
Pull the end of the line around against itself.

STEP 2
Using the loop formed, make a simple overhand loop. Keeping the two lengths of line together is the problem here – twisting the double thickness slightly can help.

STEP 3
Pull the end of the loop through a second time.

STEP 4
Tighten after moistening. The finished loop can be made smaller or larger during the tying process by gently moving the knot while tightening.

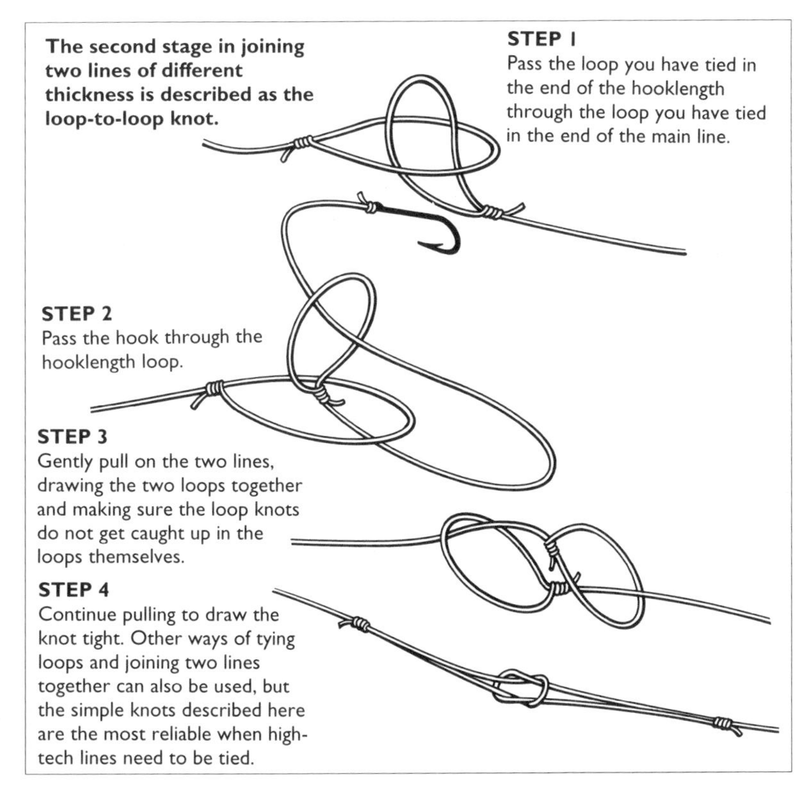

The Loop-to-loop knot

Q What is meant by the term 'balling it in'? I've often heard it mentioned by anglers talking about polefishing?

A If you're lucky enough to be able to watch a World Championship event or one of the few contests where large amounts of bloodworm and jokers are required in this country, you'll soon learn what 'balling it in' means. Basically, it is a method of feeding where several large, jaffa-sized balls of groundbait and live feed – usually jokers – are introduced right at the start of a contest, or in the special 5-minute pre-baiting period allowed in events fished to World Championship rules. Depending on the quality of the fishery and the species to be encountered, as many as 50 – yes, 50 – of these balls are thrown in by the angler who moulds them all before he throws them, and uses his pole-tip as a marker for the balls. The next ball of feed is in the air as soon as the previous one has landed on the water, but don't be surprised if he gets a bite first cast. The commotion usually has the effect of provoking the curiosity of the fish, who, having come to investigate, discover the jokers and start feeding in earnest. It's a technique that only works properly with bloodworm and jokers, and even then is best not worth bothering about on the majority of venues in this country. It's great fun to watch, though!

Q The best way of fishing a drain near where I live is by using a 10 m pole with a short line, but the problem is that the banks of the drain are very steep and unshipping is a problem as I can't push the pole back behind me. What is the answer?

A That's a good question and one faced by many anglers who fish drains and other venues with steeply sloping banks. They can usually manage to get themselves a comfortable perch with the aid of a platform so the actual fishing process is not a problem. Unshipping, however, is difficult. The best way of unshipping on a sloping bank is to strike, then quickly draw the fish away from the shoal by moving the poletip round to the side, before unshipping by pushing the pole back almost parallel with the bank. Having unshipped, you must make sure the bottom half of your pole doesn't slide into the water. You can do this by arranging your tackle so the front end of the lower half can be wedged against something like your right-hand-side bait tray, or the mouth of your keep-net. This second option – your keep-net – is a very good way of doing things as it also keeps one of your unshipping joints clean if the end of section is just in the water.

Another way of unshipping on a sloping bank is to unship a few joints at a time, while another is to plunge

Wedge the front of your unshipped section in your keepnet.

the tip of the pole in the water once you have hit the bite, giving more of an angle for the pole to be pushed up the bank. This is not recommended in shallow, clear water, however, as it will certainly scare the fish.

Q Should I prepare groundbait at home or on the riverbank?

A If you know where you are fishing the following day, it is a good idea to prepare your groundbait the night before. You'll be itching to get started, so it's great to able to pour your ready-mixed groundbait from a polythene bag into a bowl (passing it through a maggot riddle on the way if you want to) instead of spending another 10 minutes mixing it on the bank. Mixing it the night before has other advantages, in that the groundbait will absorb a lot of water, and you can make sure it is exactly the right texture – neither too dry nor too damp – before bagging it up and putting it in the fridge until the following morning. When mixing, add water a little at a time to the dry feed in a round bowl, and pass the mixed groundbait through a maggot riddle to remove any lumps. Liquidized bread for punched bread fishing, of course, must be prepared the night before, unless you have a liquidizer on the bank with you! Don't thrown away any groundbait or liquidized bread at the end of a session. Simply return it to the bag and pop it in the freezer when you get home. It will be fine for at least one more session.

Riddle mixed groundbait before using.

Q Should I leave my pole tackle in the same place every time, or should I move it about?

A One of the beauties of polefishing is its versatility. You can use a pole to keep a bait as steady as a rock, or you can constantly 'twitch' the bait by lifting the pole upwards and from side to side. In fact it is this regular movement of the bait that often prompts fish to take it. Watch a good canal angler fishing with bloodworm and he is always agitating the float, which in turn agitates the bait. A fish will often take a bait that is moving, fearing it might go away. That same fish might have ignored a stationary bait. Even on rivers, if the passage of a pole float through your swim is slowed down before releasing it again, this can spur a fish in to take it. This is a common trick employed by anglers using a stick float with rod-and-reel tackle

Regular movement of your tackle often induce a bite.

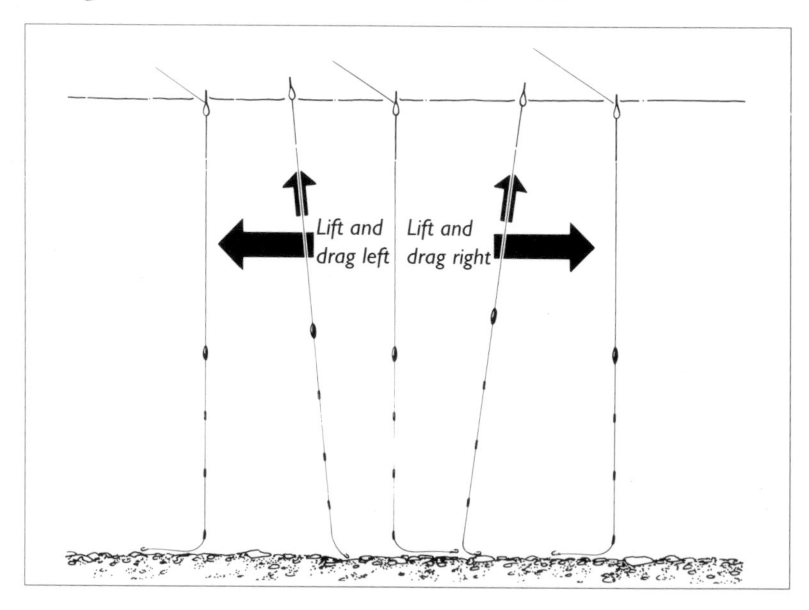

Q Is it always a good idea to start off fishing stillwaters with a pole with the bottom few inches of my pole-rig line lying on the bottom.

A As a general rule, when you're fishing in lakes, the best place to start is with your hookbait actually resting on the bottom. That's where the fish will usually be as well, and by subtle movements of the bait from side to side, you should soon start to get bites. However, with regular feeding you should soon start to see the fish coming up off the bottom. Watch for bites 'on the drop', which might be signalled by the float's failure to settle, or its disappearing as soon as the main shot has registered by settling it to its normal level. This is the time to shallow up, or even to change rigs. For fishing on the bottom, a rig with a 'bulk' in the form of an olivette or several small shot or styls fixed close together is best. Once the fish come up in the water – and the warmer it is, the more they will – it would be better to use a lighter rig with 'strung-out' shotting, carefully laying the tackle out in a straight line on the surface to give the fish no cause for suspicion.

Q Are there any occasions when I should use a waggler float attached at the bottom end only when using a long pole and short line?

A Some anglers fishing canals, especially across towards the far side with caster hookbait, prefer a short, stubby length of peacock quill attached at the bottom end only, to one attached at both the top and the bottom. In windy conditions, sometimes the wind 'catches' the line on the surface with a top and bottom float, and while one answer is to backshot with a small weight above the float to sink the line, another way is to use a bottom-end-only float, sinking as much line as possible between float and hook.

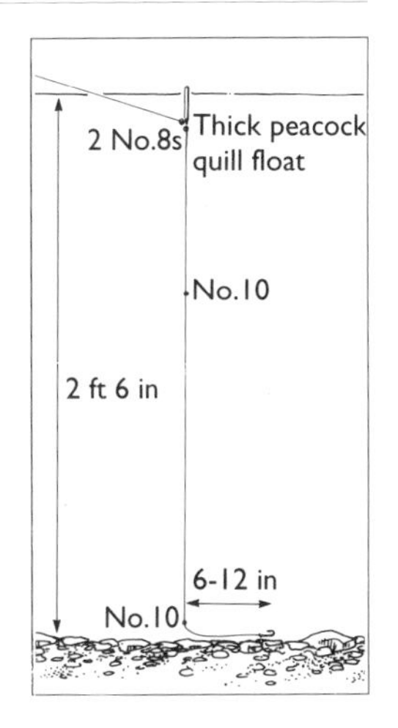

Try this rig on a canal if it's windy.

Q I've bought some pole floats that give their shotting capacity as 'four x 14' and 'four x 16'. What does this mean?

A This signifies the shotting of the float in styl weights. 'Four x 14' means that the float takes something in the region of four No.14 styls or the equivalent in order to shot it correctly. The problem here is that lead styl weights heavier than No.12 are, in fact, not allowed to be sold in this country because of problems associated with swan deaths in the 1980s. Here is a guide to what the floats would take if marked in this way:

No.13 styl – 0.625 gm
No.14 styl – 0.1 gm
No.16 styl – 0.125 gm
No.18 styl – 0.17 gm
No.20 styl – 0.31 gm

A float, taking 'four x 14' will require a weight of approximately 0.4 gm to cock it correctly.

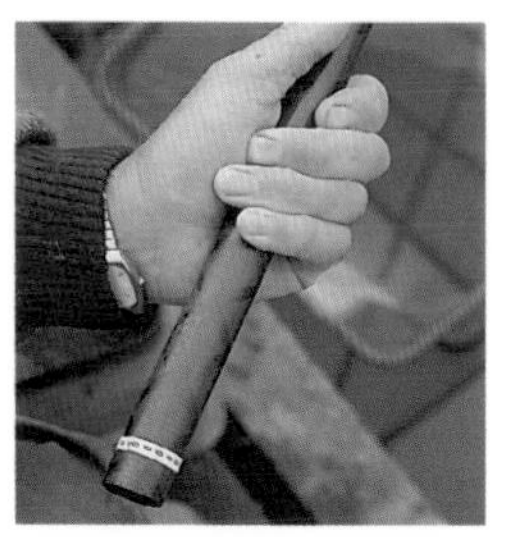

A piece of tape will ensure you unship at the right section

Q Is there any way of making sure I unship at the right section?

A Some anglers do indeed have trouble remembering which section to unship at so that a fish can be swung out safely or netted. Others get it right every time. If you're in any doubt, a dab of typewriter correcting fluid on the relevant joint will do the trick, or wrap a thin piece of white tape around it. Remember, however, that sometimes you might want to unship at the next section towards the butt of the pole, letting the elastic do its work so the fish will still be swung to hand. Try this with small chub and skimmer bream.

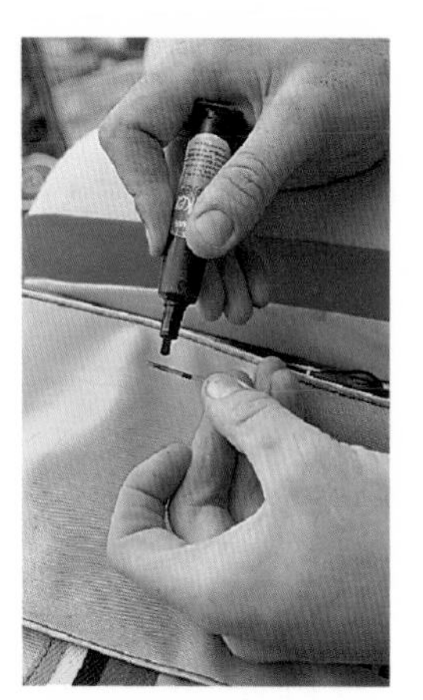

Take a black indelible felt-tip pen to change the bristle colour.

Q What is the best colour for pole-float tips? Can you change their colour during a session?

A The best colour depends on the background against which you are fishing. If you are dropping your tackle close to the far bank of a canal, the reflection will probably be dark, so use a light-coloured bristle or tip – yellow or orange. If the reflection is of the sky, however, a black bristle will be best On those awkward days when the reflection colour keeps changing because of ripples or the position of the sun in the sky, the best colour is probably orange. A thick, black waterproof pen and quick-drying fluorescent orange paint are useful additions to the pole angler's tackle – you can then change the float tip colour in seconds if the reflection changes so much that you cannot see the float properly.

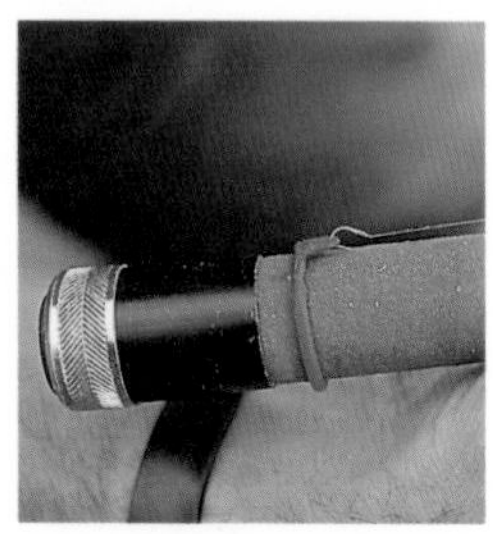

A hook-up is useful for easy storage of tackle when not in use.

Q How can I secure my hook so that it doesn't get caught up in bankside vegetation when my pole is not is use?

A One way is to hook it under the bottom of the unshipping section, but there are useful devices called 'hook-ups', which are preferred by many anglers. These are elastic bands with an extra tag with a hole at one side. They are wrapped around the pole near the bottom of the unshipping section. The hook is then slipped into this small hole and everything is neat and tidy. They're useful for whips too, where quite often the bung on the end of the whip prevents you from securing the hook there.

Signing off: Jan Porter with the fruits of three hours on the pole.

GLOSSARY OF TERMS

■ **Backshotting** – Fixing a small shot a few inches above a float to sink the line out of the way of the wind.
■ **Barbless** – Hook with no barb whatsoever.
■ **Bloodworm** – The larvae of the gnat mainly used by match anglers on difficult small-fish venues.
■ **Breaking strain** – Rough guide to the strength of a line. Line of 3 lb breaking strain will break if it tries to lift a weight of 3 lb. Use it as a guide – along with diameter – when buying line.
■ **Bulk** – Term used to described a group of shot used between float and hook to pull the bait quickly through the water.

■ **Catapult** – Essential piece of kit used by anglers to propel bait into the swim. There are many different catapult pouches to choose from, some designed to loosefeed small samples of bait like maggots and casters, others to fire out balls of groundbait.
■ **Crystal bend** – Pattern of hook favoured for maggot fishing where the bait hangs below the point.

■ **Disgorger** – Instrument used to help anglers unhook their catch. No angler should be without one.
■ **Droppers** – Small weights used close to the hook to provide a slow fall of bait in the bottom part of the water.

■ **Flick-tip** – Fine, flexible tip of a pole which is designed to avoid 'bumping' fish on the strike. An alternative to elastic, but not recommended for big fish.

■ **Gozzer** – Home-bred maggot which is very soft and favoured for bream.
■ **Groundbait** – Dry powder containing many ingredients to which sufficient water is added so it can be squeezed into balls.

■ **Hooklength** – Short length of line of less breaking strain than the main reel line, used immediately above the hook.

■ **Joker** – Midge larvae, smaller than a bloodworm, mainly used as feed on canals.

■ **Keepnet** – Net used by some anglers to retain their catch until the end of the session.

■ **Landing net** – Smaller net on the end of a pole used to lift a hooked fish from the water.
■ **Loosefeed** – The opposite of groundbait, loosefeed is 'neat' bait introduced into a swim such as maggots, caster or sweetcorn.

■ **Micro-barb** – Type of hook with a very tiny barb, less damaging to fish than a hook with a large barb and with good penetration powers.

■ **Olivette** – Pear-shaped weight used by pole anglers to get the bait down quickly through surface layers.
■ **On the drop** – A way of fishing designed to catch fish as the bait is falling through the water. Fish can be caught with float or leger tactics in this way.

■ **Pinkies** – Smaller than hook maggots, an excellent bait for feed and on the hook. A fresh pinkie is almost pure white but after a couple of days they tend to take on a pink tinge.
■ **Pole cup** – Small plastic cup fitted on the tip section of a pole which is used to deposit bait in exactly the right place.
■ **Pre-stretched** – Term used to describe some fishing lines which have been stretched as part of the manufacturing process. Pre-stretched lines are very thin, but have little elasticity.
■ **PTFE bush** – Device which is fixed to the tip of a pole allowing elastic to flow smoothly. PTFE is almost friction-free.

■ **Shank** – Part of a hook between its bend and the spade or eye.
■ **Shot** – Several sizes of spherical weight with a split which are fixed on to line to weight floats. They range in size from SSG (1.89 gms) to No 13 (0.012 gms).
■ **Squatts** – Very small maggots, good for feeding both in groundbait and loosefeeding at close range. Much used for bream feed, often with casters in groundbait.
■ **Styls** – Cylindrical weights used as an alternative to round, split shot. Attached to the line with special pincers. Much used by pole anglers.

■ **Tares** – Seed used mainly as animal feed but often irresistible to Summer roach.
■ **To-hand** – Fishing to-hand means that a pole angler is using a length of line the same as the pole or whip.
■ **Turmeric** – Bitter, orange ground spice used to flavour and colour maggots.

■ **Waggler** – Float designed for slow or still waters, attached to the line at the bottom end only and good in a wind. Most of its weight-carrying capacity is used to lock the float on the line.
■ **Water knot** – One of the best knots for joining two lengths of line, much used by anglers when legering.
■ **Weigh-in** – Weighing of each angler's catch at the end of a competition.

INDEX

OTHER TITLES AVAILABLE:

Other *Improve Your Coarse Fishing* books:

FLOAT FISHING
Edited by
Neil Pope
with a foreword by
Dave Harrell

to follow:

BAITS
LEGERING

THE ANGLING TIMES LIBRARY

with John Wilson:

- *CARP*
- *TENCH*
- *CHUB*
- *PIKE*
- *BREAM*
- *BARBEL*
- *ROACH, RUDD & DACE*